FLY THE W™

2016 WORLD CHAMPIONS

1060 West Addison Street
Chicago, IL 60613
cubs.com

Tom Ricketts
Executive Chairman

Crane Kenney
President, Business Operations

Theo Epstein
President, Baseball Operations

Colin Faulkner
SVP, Sales and Marketing

Alison Miller
VP, Marketing

Stephen Green
Principal Photographer

Ed Hartig
Team Historian

Kelly Scoggan
Executive Assistant,
Sales & Marketing

Reproduction in whole or in part without permission is prohibited.
First Edition
Copyright © 2017 All rights reserved. Chicago Cubs Baseball Club, LLC.
Printed in the United States of America by Jostens, Inc.
10 9 8 7 6 5 4 3 2 1
ISBN: 978-0-692-81345-4
Library of Congress number: 2016961026

PUBLISHED BY

9933 Alliance Road
Cincinnati, OH 45242
eminetwork.com

Lisa Lickert
President

Gary Cohen
Author/Editor-in-Chief

Phil Barnes
Author/Senior Editor

Jane Weldon
Copy Editor

Jeff Eads
Project Manager

Rick Artz
Creative Director

Bethany Nistler
Senior Designer

David Grome
Creative Consultant

This book is dedicated to the fans, front-office members, associates and players who have stood by the franchise for generations in the hopes of one day witnessing a Cubs World Series title. For every name on every brick outside of Wrigley Field, for every grandparent and parent who has passed down their love of the Cubs, for every fan who has bled Cubbie blue through the good times and bad, for every current and former player who has ever put on the blue pinstripes, and for every person who has toiled in anonymity to make this organization great, this book is for you. We thank you for your support and congratulate you on your Cubs World Series championship.

FLY THE W™

2016 WORLD CHAMPIONS

ACKNOWLEDGMENTS

It can truly be said this project was a century in the making, and, in retrospect, we wouldn't have had it any other way. Fly the W was a collaborative effort by the Cubs organization to tell the story of the magical 2016 season from start to finish. We believe ours was the most incredible journey in all of sports, spanning generations of fans who have passed their love of the franchise down through the decades. It was only appropriate that the most incredible journey in all of sports also gave us one of the most memorable and emotional finishes in the history of the game. Our goal, throughout the entire organization, has always been to reward the most dedicated fans in sports with a World Series championship. The 2016 season was the culmination of the tireless work of our players and the countless people who have supported them over the years, including all of our Cubs associates and, most importantly, our loyal fans. Sports have the power to bring people together and forge memories that will last a lifetime. While much of the 2016 season will never be forgotten, some moments will naturally fade over time. It is our hope that this book helps memorialize the historic 2016 season and provides fans an inside look at the most incredible journey in sports history.

FLY THE W

TABLE OF CONTENTS

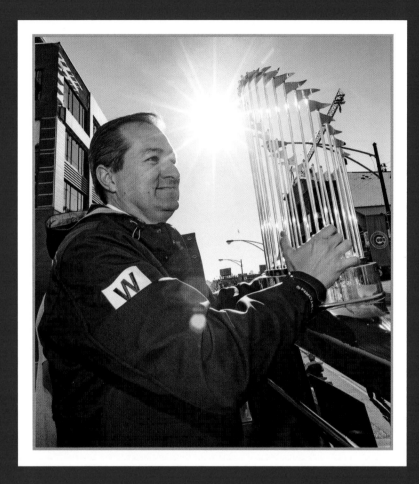

While Wrigley Field will always be perfect on a sunny summer day, we look forward to the ballpark creating lasting memories on crisp October nights for many years to come.

TOM RICKETTS

There are certain achievements in sport that are transcendent. These events are far more than just a game, a victory or a thrilling athletic feat. These accomplishments can redefine a team, turn players into legends and reward generations of fans. The Chicago Cubs' 2016 World Series victory is one of these achievements and one of the greatest stories in the history of sport.

It all begins with the best fans in the world.

Without great fans, you cannot have a great team, and the Chicago Cubs have the best fans in all of sports. A true fan base is defined by how it supports its team through thick AND thin. No team has ever had a more loyal fan base through a longer championship drought. Generations of Cubs fans were defined by our steadfast support and optimism in the face of failure and disappointment. Today, we are defined as champions.

"Game 7 of the World Series was, undoubtedly, one of the most exciting games in the history of baseball. It took extra innings to determine the winner, as both teams played with the passion and determination of true champions."

As you probably know, I walk around the ballpark almost every game. Over the past seven years, I have met literally thousands of fans in the grandstand, bleachers and out in the community. I want to personally thank everyone who took time to talk with me, give me advice or offer support. We went through some tough times together, but I hope you agree it was all worth it in the end.

Great fans deserve a great ballpark.

Wrigley Field is in a category of its own. No sporting facility in the world means so much to so many people. Wrigley is, of course, friendly, but it is also beautiful, intimate and inviting. Wrigley's charm is unique and organic. Over the past few years, we have worked hard to preserve the beauty and historic features our fans have cherished for more than a century while upgrading the overall fan experience. Your grandchildren will be able to enjoy the same comfortable and familiar setting at Wrigley Field that you and your grandparents fell in love with.

This year, Wrigley Field hosted its first World Series games in 71 years. These evenings were magical. The warm and dark tones of the ballpark and the electricity of the crowd combined to create a playoff atmosphere no one will ever forget. While Wrigley Field will always be perfect on a sunny summer day, we look forward to the ballpark creating lasting memories on crisp October nights for many years to come.

Great fans also deserve a great team.

In 2016, the most loyal fans in the best ballpark were treated to some great baseball. In fact, this past season's Cubs squad was one of the best in decades. The Cubs won 103 games in a tough division by exceling in all aspects of the game. On offense, the team consistently worked deep into counts, took walks and gathered clutch hits. The club was second in on-base percentage and scored the third-most runs in baseball. The

pitching was even better as the Cubs, by far, allowed the fewest runs in baseball and led the league in earned run average. A major part of that run prevention can be attributed to one of the best defensive seasons in baseball history.

This team was constructed from the ground up, over time, piece by piece, through the draft, free-agent signings and dozens of trades. These player acquisitions focused on players who performed on the field, but also were good teammates and of high character. Over the past few seasons, we as fans have watched many of these young men not only play baseball games, but also truly develop into great baseball players.

All these things set the stage for one of the most dramatic playoff runs in baseball history ...

Game 7 of the World Series was, undoubtedly, one of the most exciting games in the history of baseball. It took extra innings to determine the winner, as both teams played with the passion and determination of true champions. However, we should not let the last game of the playoff run make us forget the drama of the National League Division Series and National League Championship Series. Each of these matchups had its own storylines, with failure and frustration followed by moments of success and redemption.

It began with the San Francisco Giants.

The Cubs had a few days off as we waited for the winner of the National League

Wild Card Game. On Oct. 7, the Giants came to Wrigley Field for the first game of the NLDS. San Francisco came in with the momentum of the Wild Card win and having won seven of their last 10 games. They also were a proven, playoff-tested, veteran team that had won the World Series in each of the three previous "even" years.

The series started with a classic pitching duel. A solo homer proved to be the only run. The Cubs jumped out to a four-run lead in Game 2 and held on to take a two-games-to-none lead in the series. Then things moved to the Bay, where the Cubs lost a 13-inning thriller in Game 3. After being held in check for the first eight innings of Game 4, the Cubs rallied for four runs in the ninth, in one of the most dramatic comebacks in postseason history, to clinch the series three games to one.

"I was there and know it all happened, and yet, at times, it still doesn't seem real. The Cubs won the 2016 World Series. They did it for and with the best fans in all of sport. They did it while calling the best ballpark in baseball home. And they did it with a dramatic postseason run that will never be forgotten."

Then came the Los Angeles Dodgers.

The following weekend, the Cubs hosted the Dodgers at Wrigley Field. Los Angeles came in having won their division by four games, despite an incredible string of injuries that included missing one of the best pitchers in baseball, Clayton Kershaw, for a large part of the season. They, too, were ready after vanquishing the Washington Nationals in their National League Division Series.

The Dodgers series began well for the Cubs, with a dramatic, eighth-inning, pinch-hit grand slam by Miguel Montero providing the difference in an 8-4 win. The Dodgers arms got the best of the Cubs in Games 2 and 3, as they twirled back-to-back shutouts. Trailing in the series, the Cubs bats came alive, as this resilient group bounced back for three consecutive

convincing wins to clinch the team's first National League pennant since 1945.

And the stage was set for the World Series.

The American League champion Cleveland Indians racked up 94 regular-season wins and had convincingly won both of their playoff series. The Indians were both hot and well rested as the Cubs went to Cleveland on Oct. 25 to begin one of the most dramatic World Series in baseball history.

Despite the Cubs coming in as favorites, the Indians were indeed ready for the challenge and played their way to a 3-1 series lead behind strong pitching. The Cubs had their backs to the wall. To win, they would need to become only the fifth team in World Series history to overcome such a deficit. With elimination on the line, Game 5 was a tense affair, as the bullpen protected a one-run lead over the final three innings. Game 6 was an offensive display highlighted by a fourth-inning Addison Russell grand slam.

It is possible there may come a time when I can think and write about Game 7 without getting emotional—I am not at that point yet. The elation of establishing an early lead gave way to the tension of protecting that lead. I was as stunned as any fan when the Indians tied the game with an unlikely home run in the eighth inning. Then the briefest of rain delays set the stage for an indescribable 10th inning. As the whole nation watched,

the Cubs scored twice and held off one last push by the Indians to close out the series. It was one of the greatest games of all time.

I was there and know it all happened, and yet, at times, it still doesn't seem real. The Cubs won the 2016 World Series. They did it for and with the best fans in all of sport. They did it while calling the best ballpark in baseball home. And they did it with a dramatic postseason run that will never be forgotten.

There are certain achievements in sport that are transcendent. This was one of them.

Tom

— Tom Ricketts
Executive Chairman

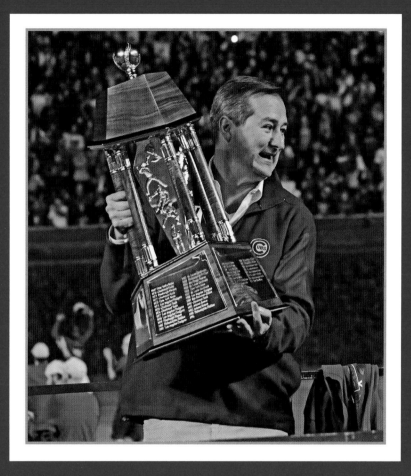

It is possible there may come a time when I can think and write about Game 7 without getting emotional—I am not at that point yet.

"There were times, as
the players answered
every challenge and
performed at such
an elite level for so
long, when I was in
awe of this team."

— THEO EPSTEIN —

I saw, through the window of the weight room door, the backs of our players' blue jerseys, shoulder to shoulder and packed tightly, all 25 guys squeezed into a space designed for half that many.

THEO EPSTEIN

Like everyone else who cared about the Cubs, I was in a daze. A three-run lead in Game 7 with four outs to go, nobody on, bottom of the order coming up—and it was gone in the blink of an eye. The stunning homer by Rajai Davis was impossible to process in real time. We sat silent, shaken and surrounded by the thunderous roar of the home crowd. The ninth inning only added more angst, with the pain of stranding the winning run at third and the anxiety of watching an exhausted Aroldis Chapman somehow get three outs.

Then the rain came and the tarp was pulled, providing just enough of a pause to ponder the magnitude of the situation. Extra innings in Game 7 of the World Series. An entire season, down to this one moment. One hundred and three wins and 10 more in the playoffs, down to this. Eight and a half months of grind since reporting to spring training, down to this. Five years of build, sweat and tears, down to this. One hundred and eight years of love and patience, down to this.

"This was a team of young players, mature beyond their years, who cut their teeth in the middle of pennant races in 2015 and 2016."

En route to a basement suite to meet with Major League Baseball about the weather, I made my way through our clubhouse, still trying to come to grips with all that hung in the balance and the three-run lead that no longer was. Turning a corner, I saw, through the window of the weight room door, the backs of our players' blue jerseys, shoulder to shoulder and packed tightly, all 25 guys squeezed into a space designed for half that many. It was an unusual sight. We hardly ever had meetings and never during a game. Was this a group lament? A bitch session? A last-minute strategic meeting? Did someone pass out?

None of that would have fit the personality of the 2016 Cubs. This was a group of players as connected to one another and to the fans as I have ever seen. They liked each other, hung out together, challenged each other, dreamed together, persevered together, dominated together. All year long, they were keenly aware of how much talent was in that clubhouse, what an opportunity they had and how badly the fans wanted it.

These are the players who showed up to spring training having already thought through how they would handle the grand expectations and the target on their backs. They said they wanted to get off to a great start and maintained amazing focus and intensity in roaring to 26 wins in the first 31 games. They maintained humility and perspective when the national media started to write about the '27 Yankees, the '01 Mariners and the all-time wins record. During the season's only hiccup, a tough three-week stretch at the end of the first half when mental and physical fatigue kicked in, they kept saying they just needed to get to the All-Star break. Sure enough, they raced out of the break, winning 20 of the first 26 games on the way to a 50-23 second half.

This was a team of young players, mature beyond their years, who cut their teeth in the middle of pennant races in 2015 and 2016. They cared not about looking cool or fitting in but about winning, and that won over the veterans, young and old, who helped them belong and helped show them the way. To say I trusted and respected this team is an understatement. There were times, as the players answered every challenge and performed at such an elite level for so long, when I was in awe of this team.

I looked through the window and scanned the weight room. Brothers in blue jerseys, shoulder to shoulder.

There was Anthony Rizzo, among the first to arrive via trade when he was a 21-year-old coming off a disastrous major-league debut. He grinded his way through the lean years, establishing himself as a star and waiting for the rest of the talent to join him. Now, at 27, he was the de facto captain who had come to embody the overall talent and personality of the team. He overcame a rough start to the postseason to deliver big hit after big hit against the Dodgers and Indians. He loved his teammates, especially the retiring David Ross, and he loved the fans. He had been talking about winning the World Series for them all year.

There was Kris Bryant, on his way to the NL MVP Award. From the circus surrounding his debut to the Rookie of the Year Award to meeting all the expectations of his sophomore season, he always handled himself with grace and, at 24, was already one of the best players in the game. But he never played with more passion than he did in this postseason. He hit big home runs: the shocking ninth-inning blast to tie Game 3 at San Francisco, the drought-ending homer off Trevor Bauer in Game 5 of the World Series and the first-inning shot off Josh Tomlin at Cleveland to set the tone in Game 6. And he ran the bases with passion and precision, scoring early in the seventh game from first on Rizzo's single and then from third on Addison Russell's short sacrifice fly. For a player who normally hides his emotions on the field, his face showed how much fun he was having and how much he wanted to win the series.

There was David Ross, in the final game of both his respected career and his remarkable two-year stint with the Cubs, in which, as a backup catcher, he captured the hearts of his teammates and the fan base. Ross was the glue, so thoughtful about all the ingredients that create winning, from the fundamentals and strategy on the field to the relationships and conversations off it. He had homered earlier in the game and was leading the team in slugging during the postseason. This was his last game, and his teammates knew it.

There was Kyle Schwarber, who should not have even been playing after his horrific knee injury but somehow returned and was raking as always. He never left the team during his rehab, getting his grueling work done early and then finding ways to contribute, from breaking down video to providing moral support on the bench. He stayed connected and came back early for his teammates and for his organization. The only thing missing from the 2016 season had been restored: Schwarber was in the lineup and helping his team win. He had a bat in his hands at the meeting, getting ready to lead off the 10th inning.

"*There, in the middle of it all, was Jason Heyward, who, I would later learn, had called the meeting.*"

There was Jon Lester, who believed in this vision for a young championship Cubs team when it was still just a last-place club with a lot of prospects. He worked hard, prepared and led by example, pitching at an elite level for two years. In this postseason, his poise and pressure pitching changed the tone of each series: in NLDS Game 1, in NLCS Games 1 and 5, and in the tense fifth game of the World Series at Wrigley Field. He had gutted through his first relief appearance in nine years an hour earlier. He was so close to seeing the vision realized.

There was Jake Arrieta, who had turned his career around as a Cub, becoming one of the best pitchers in baseball. He had already won Games 2 and 6, and had his spikes on, having already warmed up, at the ready to pitch out of the bullpen.

There was Kyle Hendricks, who had pitched his heart out hours earlier. He had grown so much since coming over in a trade as a Sin-

gle-A pitcher, grown even since the playoffs the previous year. A Cy Young favorite, he was spellbindingly good all year, including his masterpiece against the Dodgers to win the pennant. He had given all he could.

There was Ben Zobrist, as steady and selfless in the postseason as ever. He moved to left field to get Javier's glove to second and played brilliantly in left. He had already changed the fortunes of both previous series with big hits: a double in the epic ninth-inning rally against the Giants and a leadoff bunt single in the fourth inning of Game 4 against the Dodgers that ended the teamwide slump and opened the floodgates. He wanted one more big at-bat.

There was Dexter Fowler, our leadoff man. He led off spring training with his surprise return into the welcoming arms of teammates and friends. He led off the season by carrying the club through a prodigious April. He led off Game 7 with a home run. He had come back to finish the job.

There was Javier Baez, who had carried the team through the first two rounds with his incredible all-around play. In the World Series, he had struggled, swinging wildly and making a pair of errors early in Game 7. As he always does, he redeemed himself, hitting a big home run in the fifth. He had come so far, and he was so close.

There was Addison Russell, as calm as ever since taking over shortstop as a 21-year-old in August of 2015 in the middle of a pennant race. He too had overcome some early playoff struggles, playing flawless defense and hitting three huge home

runs, including the grand slam that effectively ended Game 6 the night before.

There was Willson Contreras, who as a rookie caught some of the biggest wins in franchise history and played with passion on every pitch. On June 17, on the first pitch he saw as a big leaguer, he homered. In the fourth inning of Game 7, on the last pitch of his season, he doubled off the wall to put the Cubs up two runs.

There was Miguel Montero, who didn't care about his batting average. He had his mind only on winning and the chance to contribute one more big hit.

There was John Lackey, who had come to the Cubs only for jewelry.

There was Chapman, one of the best closers ever and the hero of Game 5, acquired to record the final outs in series like these. He had done so against the Giants and the Dodgers, but he already knew he would not on this night. He had willed his way through a scoreless ninth but was distraught, no matter how often his teammates told him they wouldn't be there without him.

There were Carl Edwards Jr. and Mike Montgomery, a 48th-round pick and an out-of-options reliever before being traded to the Cubs. Edwards had two career saves, and Montgomery had none. They had no way to know they were both about to be called upon to close out a World Series.

There, in the middle of it all, was Jason Heyward, who, I would later learn, had called the meeting. Through his long season with the bat, he never stopped playing great defense, never stopped running the bases, and never

There was Kyle Schwarber, who should not have even been
playing after his horrific knee injury but somehow returned and
was raking as always.

"We win it right here!" was the last thing I heard walking away.
Ten minutes later, we did.

stopped being a great teammate. Most players in down years hide, or isolate themselves, or even disappear. But here was Heyward, as respected as anyone in the clubhouse, stepping forward to lead when the team stared at the kind of adversity as a group he had faced as an individual all year.

This was the team that scored four in the ninth at San Francisco when staring down Johnny Cueto in an elimination game.

This was the team that stormed back to win three in a row over the Dodgers, the last against Clayton Kershaw, to claim the pennant.

This was the team that chanted "we never quit" after every game.

Now, before extra innings in the biggest game they will ever play in, the players gathered in the dank weight room. The door was ajar, and I lingered just long enough to hear a few words.

"We are the best team in baseball!" shouted one of the players.

"We've got you, Chappy, we've got you!" said another.

"We've worked so hard all year just for this moment."

"This is only going to make it sweeter, boys!"

"Keep grinding, keep grinding!"

I turned and headed to the weather meeting, smiling and reassured. *"We win it right here!"* was the last thing I heard walking away. Ten minutes later, we did.

Schwarber, who had been in the Arizona Fall League 10 days earlier, smoked a leadoff single through the right side. Then, Albert Almora, who as a 17-year-old in 2012 had teared up in his family's living room while pledging how badly he wanted a chance to help the Cubs win a World Series, made a game-changing play. Bryant hit a deep fly to right-center, and Almora, reading his fellow center fielder's gait, knew Davis would catch it and retreated to first to tag and advance. Three consecutive first-round draft picks combined to get the possible World Series-winning run into scoring position.

Things started to happen in slow motion after that. Zobrist's double down the line and leap into second base. Rizzo's disbelief. Montero's big single. CJ's two outs. A walk, a hit, a run. Montgomery trotting in. A curveball for strike one. Another curve, a topped grounder, Bryant coming over, his plant foot slipping out from underneath him …

So many thoughts and emotions swirled through my head as Rizzo caught the ball and thrust his hands in the air—joy, relief and the realization that so many deserving people had just become World Champions:

» the players, who stood shoulder to shoulder in the weight room and all year, and made it happen;

» the Ricketts family, led by Tom, who could not have been more patient or supportive, and who had spent long nights during the rebuild walking through the upper deck, passing out baseballs, rain or shine, loss after loss;

» Joe and the coaches, who created a culture of authenticity, preparedness, connection, perseverance, fun and excellence;

» the 120 baseball ops staffers who had crowded into a Mesa hotel conference room for four days in 2011 deciding how we would play the game, how we would teach the game, what we would stand for, what would be The Cubs Way;

» Jed and Jason, my baseball brothers, who walked away from great jobs in San Diego for a chance to reunite and make history together again in Chicago;

» the player development staff, who were the first ones to start to change the culture and define what it meant to be a Cub;

» the pro scouts, analysts and front-office guys, who pulled all-nighters and helped trade for Rizzo, Hendricks, Arrieta, Russell, Fowler, Montero, Edwards, Montgomery and Chapman;

» the amateur scouts, who delivered Baez, Almora, Schwarber and Bryant;

» the international staff, cheering at our academy, who had signed Soler, Contreras and many others on the way;

» Ernie, Ronnie, Billy, Fergie, Ryne, Sut, Kerry, Demp and everyone who has ever put on a Cubs uniform;

» and our wonderful fans, most deserving of all, whose love was finally rewarded.

Two days later, our players assembled on the stage at Grant Park, facing the fans with whom they felt such a special connection. This was likely the last time they would ever be together as a group in full. I stood off to the side of the stage and admired them. They stood shoulder to shoulder again, celebrating the great things they had accomplished for each other and for the millions who were smiling back at them. I was still in awe of this team—and I know I always will be.

— Theo Epstein
President, Baseball Operations

"For a week, hope reigned. And while maybe not another Miracle on Ice, I'll defend the idea that the world actually stopped spinning in Chicago for at least a moment. The Cubs won the World Series."

— CRANE KENNEY —

According to the Mayor's office, at least 5 million people showed up for our victory parade. That gathering was the seventh-largest collection of human beings in history and the largest ever in the Western Hemisphere.

CRANE KENNEY

About a week after the World Series parade, I found myself quoting the great American philosopher Yogi Berra: "It's like déjà vu all over again."

Everybody my age knows where they were in 1980, when a group of scrappy American college kids bested the unbeatable Soviet hockey team in Lake Placid. The Cold War had not yet ended, Americans were being held hostage in Iran, and our country was in an awful recession. On that day, regardless of your interest in hockey or the Olympics, the world stopped spinning, and every American shouted something like "Holy cow! They did it." That game gave us a break, and we celebrated a moment of national pride. It has since become known as the Miracle on Ice.

"Our beloved ballpark is also the connection for generations of people. Never was that more true than in 2016, when our fans turned Wrigley Field into a dynamic, living memorial. I noticed the first chalk tribute after we beat the Dodgers in Game 6 of the NLCS to reach the World Series for the first time since 1945."

I've used that story as a recruiting pitch for 10 years with potential new associates, corporate sponsors, media partners and others. Our prediction was that the next time the sports world stopped spinning would be when the Cubs won the World Series. And the hook has always been: "Don't you want to be a part of it?"

According to the Mayor's office, at least 5 million people showed up for our victory parade. That gathering was the seventh-largest collection of human beings in history and the largest ever in the Western Hemisphere. I haven't seen evidence the world actually stopped spinning in November, but I would bet this season and these players will vault to the forefront of the history books for Cubs fans, no matter how many titles and parades happen in the future.

And our fans are amazing historians. They can remember details of their first game, where they stood for an important home run, the foul ball caught by their father, a comeback win and who was with them on each occasion. Those who attended the first Wrigley Field World Series in 71 years will recall Jon Lester's guts in Game 5. Nobody will forget Kris Bryant's homer or Aroldis Chapman's eight-out save in that same game. And they will surely recall how Wrigley Field looked, sounded, smelled and shook.

For most of us, Wrigley Field is not just a ballpark. Fans have told me it's their summer home. Some call it their country club. Those playing hooky from work call it their office. As we all know, Ernie Banks famously called it the Friendly Confines. This year, Joe Maddon said Wrigley was "the essence of baseball." Ben Zobrist called it "baseball heaven on earth." And Bill Murray described seeing Wrigley Field on only black-and-white TV until his brother Brian took him to his first game when he was 7 years old. He said his brother covered his eyes until he walked to the top of the stairs and then, "There was this beautiful grass and this beautiful ivy. I'd only seen it in black and white. I was a blind man made to see."

Our beloved ballpark is also the connection for generations of people. Never was that more true than in 2016, when our fans turned Wrigley Field into a dynamic, living memorial. I noticed the first chalk tribute after we beat the Dodgers in Game 6 of the NLCS to reach the World Series for the first time since 1945. In blue chalk, at about eye level, someone had written, "Dad—Here we go. World Series 2016."

More messages went up daily, and by the time we got back from Cleveland on Thursday morning, the walls were covered. Hundreds of people were hard at work, standing on stepladders to find open canvas or crouching to ant level to add to the mosaic.

Most messages were aimed above. Mine was the same: "For Ernie, Ron, Jack, Harry, Arne and Jim."

It felt great to inscribe the names of some of the men who helped make this possible. They are the ones who connected our fans to this ballpark, either by playing the game with Hall of Fame ability or by bringing it to 70 million WGN viewers outside Chicago. They put the Cubs and Wrigley Field on the world's bucket list. Because of them, we could take the risk of rebuilding both the ballpark and the team to chase a title. We know our place as caretakers of their legacy and think about them often. And, boy, how they would have loved the 2016 season.

After 23 years working toward this goal, and 23 years imagining what this moment would feel like, what a

surprise that the chalk walls would be one of my most lasting impressions. Every day, we in the front office took laps around the ballpark to see the additions from the previous night. The energy from the chalk walls was real. People came from all over the country to share their stories. For a week, there were a million smiles, lots of tears, photographs and laughter. Even Mother Nature seemed to be in on it, as the weather was unseasonably warm and dry. It was like time stopped. November felt like August. Grown men cried like babies. Memories were restored. We were all kids again.

Something very special happened, both on and off the field in 2016. The beauty of the chalk walls was that they were organic, peaceful, cross-generational, multi-ethnic, gender-blind and positive. The words and medium were amazingly respectful. Chalk does not hurt Wrigley Field.

One couldn't help but contrast this unscripted movement with the other big stories of the day. It was like Cubs fans decided to take a collective time-out from the nationally divisive presidential election, our insolvent state being run without a budget and the senseless loss of young lives that was occurring locally.

For a week, hope reigned. And while maybe not another Miracle on Ice, I'll defend the idea that the world actually stopped spinning in Chicago for at least a moment. The Cubs won the World Series. Holy cow!

— Crane Kenney
President, Business Operations

FOUNDATION FOR
SUCCESS

HOW THEO EPSTEIN'S FRONT
OFFICE GROUP TOOK THE CUBS
FROM WORST TO FIRST

It was a long and winding road from Mike Quade to Joe Maddon, Aramis Ramirez to Kris Bryant, Ryan Dempster to Jon Lester. In fact, you could easily begin the epic journey a century ago, when Frank Chance's 1908 Cubs captured the organization's previous World Series title behind legends like Johnny Evers, Joe Tinker and Mordecai "Three Finger" Brown.

But the franchise's most recent iteration—the one that brought the longest-standing championship drought in American professional sports to an end by capturing a World Series title in the morning hours of Nov. 3, 2016—laid its foundations in 2011. That season, Quade's Cubs finished with a 71-91 record, leaving them mired in fifth place in the NL Central. The squad's performance led to the dismissal of general manager Jim Hendry on July 22, 2011, and cleared the way for perhaps the ideal candidate to reshape a foundering franchise—former Boston wunderkind Theo Epstein.

After 10 years with the Red Sox, a team that ended an 86-year title drought of its own under Epstein's watch in 2004, the talented GM departed Boston in 2011. When Cubs Chairman Tom Ricketts asked around to find out who would be best suited to lead the Cubs into the future, one name continually came to the forefront: Epstein.

"We were looking for someone with a background in player development, someone who had a proven track record of success, someone who had a strong analytical background and someone who had experience in creating a culture of winning," Ricketts said. "It was also important to me that this person would not be someone who was content with their past successes, but someone who would build on those successes to improve themselves and improve the organization that they're with."

Epstein was officially introduced as president of baseball operations on Oct. 25, 2011, and he immediately made it clear he was undaunted by the task ahead.

"I don't believe in curses, and I guess I played a small part in proving they don't exist, from a baseball standpoint," Epstein said, after taking the job. "I do think we can be honest and up-front that certain organizations haven't gotten the job done. That's the approach we took in Boston. We identified certain things that we hadn't been doing well that might have gotten in the way of a World Series and eradicated them. That's what we'll do here."

One of Epstein's first moves was to beef up his baseball operations team, a lean department under previous management groups. He brought over former Boston mates Jed Hoyer and Jason McLeod from San Diego to serve as his executive vice president and general manager, and senior vice president of player development and amateur scouting, respectively. Once on board, that trio went about constructing what they called a "scouting and player development machine."

"We're going to build the best baseball operation we can," Epstein said. "We're going to change the culture. Our players are going to change the culture along with us in the major-league clubhouse. We're going to make building a foundation for sustained success a priority. That will lead to playing October baseball more often than not."

At the same time, under president Crane Kenney, the Cubs business side was working to ensure the future viability of both the organization and Wrigley Field. The Cubs added new, state-of-the-art training facilities in both the Dominican Republic and Arizona. In 2014, they also kicked off the 1060 Project, a massive restoration of Wrigley Field, giving the franchise the best facilities in the game and the resources to make key baseball moves.

Still, the organization didn't turn on a dime. The Cubs won 61 games in Epstein's first year and 66 in his second under manager Dale Sveum. But the front-office team was also building the minor-league system into a juggernaut. During the Cubs' win-now run in 2007-08, the farm system had been depleted, but the new group capitalized on trades, draft picks and the international market to acquire high-upside talent quickly.

Over the years, they made trades for foundational players such as Anthony Rizzo (Padres), Jake Arrieta (Orioles), Kyle Hendricks

(Rangers), Addison Russell (Athletics) and many others. Through the MLB Draft, they picked up Bryant (2013) and Kyle Schwarber (2014). They made a savvy move to acquire reliever Hector Rondon from the Indians through the annual Rule 5 draft. On the international market, they signed players like Jorge Soler.

The improvement wasn't immediate, but it was steady. In 2011, *Baseball America* ranked the Cubs farm system 16th in baseball. By 2015, the organization's young talent was ranked first.

Once they had a core of dynamic, young, everyday players, they decided it was time to turn the corner and start acting like the big-market team they ultimately are. In a surprising turn of events following the 2014 season, the Epstein group dismissed its second manager, Rick Renteria, after one season because they had an opportunity to bring in veteran skipper Joe Maddon, a proven winner who was available only because an opt-out clause in his Rays contract was triggered when Tampa's top executive, Andrew Friedman, departed for the Dodgers.

After that, they turned their sights to the free-agent market. That same offseason, the Cubs made a strong push to land former Red Sox ace Lester, considered by many to be the top available arm. They signed Jason Heyward, Ben Zobrist and John Lackey the following year.

It was a long journey from 101 losses in 2012 to a World Series title in 2016, but through the dedication of the front office, the Cubs now have the foundation for sustained success Epstein talked about in 2011. After back-to-back postseason runs and the franchise's first World Series title in more than a century, the Cubs' future looks exceedingly bright. ●

Infielder Javier Baez, a 2011 first-round pick, is one of the few holdovers from the previous Jim Hendry front office.

Catcher Willson Contreras is the longest-tenured Cubs player on the big-league roster, having signed with the team in 2009 as an infielder.

President of Baseball Operations Theo Epstein, Senior Vice President of Player Development and Amateur Scouting Jason McLeod, Executive Vice President and General Manager Jed Hoyer and Cubs Chairman Tom Ricketts are all smiles at Wrigley Field.

Dale Sveum led a rebuilding Cubs club to a 127-197 record from 2012-13.

Rick Renteria went 73-89 in his lone season as Cubs manager in 2014.

Current Cubs manager Joe Maddon took the helm on Nov. 2, 2014, following nine seasons with the Tampa Bay Rays.

Theo Epstein's front office made outfielder Albert Almora Jr. its first top pick, in the 2012 MLB Draft.

In 2012, the Cubs inked Cuban defector and international free-agent outfielder Jorge Soler to a nine-year contract.

Following the 2012 season, the Cubs grabbed unheralded reliever Hector Rondon in the Rule 5 Draft from the Cleveland Indians.

The Cubs selected Kris Bryant with the second-overall pick of the 2013 MLB Draft. He captured the NL Rookie of the Year Award in 2015, hitting .275 with 26 homers and 99 RBI.

With the fourth-overall pick of the 2014 MLB Draft, the Cubs selected Kyle Schwarber.

One of the first major trades Theo Epstein's front office made was acquiring first baseman Anthony Rizzo for starter Andrew Cashner on Jan. 6, 2012.

In one of the most lopsided deals in recent memory, the Cubs acquired Jake Arrieta, along with reliever Pedro Strop, for Scott Feldman and Steve Clevenger on July 2, 2013. Arrieta won the NL Cy Young Award in 2015.

In parts of five seasons with Texas and Baltimore, Pedro Strop posted a 4.14 ERA. Things changed in Chicago.

Kyle Hendricks was the big return in a deal that sent starter Ryan Dempster to the Rangers on July 31, 2012. Many viewed him as nothing more than a potential fifth starter.

On July 5, 2014, Addison Russell came to the Cubs as part of a deal that sent pitchers Jeff Samardzija and Jason Hammel to Oakland.

The Cubs acquired Dexter Fowler in a Jan. 19, 2015, trade with the Astros and then re-signed him prior to the 2016 season.

On Oct. 11, 2014, the Cubs broke ground on the 1060 Project, the long-awaited expansion and restoration of Wrigley Field.

The acquisition of Jon Lester in December 2014 signaled a major turning point for the Cubs franchise.

During the Winter Meetings in 2015, the Cubs inked veteran utilityman Ben Zobrist to a four-year deal.

Joe [Maddon] was always buzzing about Jason [Heyward], about how much he impacted the game. Every time he looked at something on the field, Jason was a part of it. That's the kind of player we wanted to bring onto our team—bring into our young core.

— JED HOYER —

Seeking a final starter to round out the rotation, the Cubs signed veteran righty John Lackey on Dec. 8, 2015.

Following the 2015 season, the Cubs made another big splash, signing free-agent outfielder Jason Heyward to an eight-year deal.

SPRING TRAINING

THE STACKED CUBS LEARN TO EMBRACE THE TARGET IN MESA

Heading into spring training, the message from manager Joe Maddon was clear: Embrace the target. As the team journeyed to Mesa, Arizona, to get ready for the 2016 season, that concept would be put to the test in a major way.

After winning 97 games and making a surprising run all the way to the National League Championship Series in 2015, the Cubs bolstered their young core by signing free agents Jason Heyward, John Lackey and Ben Zobrist. Nearly every baseball expert picked the club to capture the National League pennant, and some Las Vegas oddsmakers had them as 3:1 favorites to win the World Series. The Cubs were the talk of baseball. A target was squarely on their backs.

"I'm really a big believer in running toward the fire as opposed to away from it," Maddon said as the team reported to Mesa. "I really want our guys to get comfortable with the concept of everybody speaking so glowingly of us and embracing the target.

"The target has gotten bigger. We have to embrace the target, and, while you're doing that, understand what that means."

So just how were the young Cubs planning to handle these elevated expectations? Perhaps unsurprisingly, it was business as usual—which, for a Maddon-led team, meant a disco-era dress-up day, DJs at morning stretching sessions and Munenori Kawasaki performing an Aerosmith-inspired karaoke.

Despite all the fun, when it was time to get to work, the team took its Cactus League responsibilities seriously. The Cubs' expansive Mesa compound was abuzz with major- and minor-league players doing back-to-basics drills, taking batting practice, loosening their arms and getting in shape for the grind of the regular season.

That's not to say there weren't surprises. In fact, there was a bombshell so big it shook up the baseball landscape.

On Feb. 25, a few weeks into spring training, Chicago favorite Dexter Fowler strolled onto the Sloan Park practice field while play-ers were gathered for a "morning meeting." Most around the game believed Fowler had signed a multiyear pact with Baltimore just a day earlier, but President of Baseball Operations Theo Epstein had actually orchestrated a deal to bring the center fielder and leadoff man back into the fold for one more year. Fowler broke the news to his teammates in person, and they mobbed him as if he'd just launched a walk-off homer onto Waveland Avenue.

"My heart's here," Fowler said. "I feel like the Cubs, they treated me with the utmost respect. With the offseason moves they made, you've got to go with what's comfortable."

Given the modern, social media-fueled baseball landscape, it's nearly impossible to keep anything secret these days. Still, the Fowler signing managed to catch most everyone off guard.

"[I] ran into Theo yesterday, and he said, 'Hey, I got a surprise for you guys,'" said first baseman Anthony Rizzo. "But when someone says they have a surprise, you think elephant, giraffe. You don't know. That was the last thing on my mind."

The other big story of the spring season was backup catcher David Ross' impending exit from the game. The then-15-year veteran announced during the winter that 2016 would be his final campaign, citing a desire to spend more time with his family. Despite serving as a reserve player for the majority of his career, the clubhouse stalwart was rewarded with a season-long sendoff, starting in February.

On one memorable March morning, Ross walked out to the practice field to find a rascal scooter with his name (literally) on it parked near the entrance. The transportation device, generally reserved for senior citizens, had customized license plates bearing the catcher's name and uniform number. Young teammates Kris Bryant and Rizzo also created the @grandparossy_3 Instagram account to chronicle the veteran's final year in pinstripes.

"When you're in spring training, things are nice and lighthearted and fun," Ross said. "I don't know much about social media. I'll try to do the best I can. They pretty much make fun of me, but I get on them pretty hard around here."

From elder statesmen to highly anticipated newcomers, this team had it all. Heyward, signed to an eight-year deal, was the marquee offseason acquisition and one of the most coveted free agents on the market. Coming off a fine season with the Cardinals, the versatile Gold Glove-winning outfielder was initially projected to slide into center field from his traditional right until the Cubs landed Fowler.

"Knowing the core is young and those guys are going to be around for a while is very exciting," Heyward said. "I don't want to take the highest dollar amount when my gut is telling me to go somewhere else.

"Being 26 years old and knowing that my contract would put me in any clubhouse for longer than most people there, you have to look at age, how fast the team is changing and how soon those changes will come about."

The Cubs also bolstered the veteran presence on the club by signing super-utilityman Zobrist to a four-year deal. His willingness to play all over the field, World Series bona fides with the Royals, and strong relationship with Maddon added a new dimension to the team and strengthened the clubhouse culture.

Veteran Lackey also filled an organizational need for playoff-tested starting pitching. The right-hander was brought in to be a reliable part of the regular-season rotation, but his eight previous trips to the postseason and two World Series rings made him invaluable to a young squad with championship aspirations.

These Cubs were ready to roll as they headed to Anaheim, California, for Opening Day on April 4. ◐

Dexter Fowler surprises the baseball world by deciding to re-sign with the Cubs during spring training in 2016.

Kyle Schwarber gets shaved for Joe Maddon's Respect Bald fundraiser event.

Before team stretch in Mesa each day, strength and conditioning coordinator Tim Buss gathers the team for a little fun.

"You never take anything for granted. You never get complacent. Coming off a really good season, there's a lot to be proud of, but there's so much more to accomplish."

— JOE MADDON —

During the spring, many expected Kyle Hendricks to have to battle for the fifth starter job. But the right-hander used a solid Cactus League performance as a catapult to a breakout 2016 season.

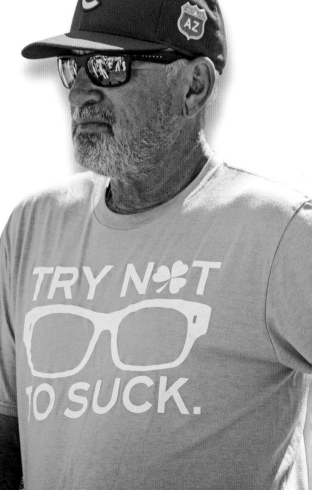

Traveling secretary Vijay Tekchandani sports disco attire after Joe Maddon brought his 1970s van onto the practice field.

Newcomer Ben Zobrist was a key offseason acquisition coming off a successful World Series run with the Royals in 2015.

To celebrate David Ross' retirement following the 2016 season, Cubs players pitched in to buy "Grandpa" a motorized scooter with personalized plates.

Dexter Fowler rounds the bases during a March 17 game at Sloan Park. Early in the 2015 season, Joe Maddon coined the phrase "You go, we go," referencing how the Cubs offense works best when Fowler sets the table for the heart of the order.

Javier Baez impressed during spring training, setting the stage for a breakout season.

Addison Russell and David Ross celebrate their win in the team relay-throw competition. Ben Zobrist and Jorge Soler were also on their team.

The Cubs finished the Cactus League season with an 11-19 record.

Pedro Strop and Javier Baez keep things light in the dugout.

John Lackey and Jon Lester discuss their live batting practice sessions on Sloan Park's main field.

Starter Jason Hammel throws an early-morning side session.

Team mascot Clark the Cub makes a spring visit to Sloan Park.

Javier Baez calls time after sliding into second during the Cubs' Cactus League home opener.

Infielder Munenori Kawasaki is reminded to Respect 90 in the tunnel on his way to the Sloan Park dugout.

> *I think if you don't set your expectations high, if you don't write your goals down and make them lofty or crazy or record-breaking goals, then you shouldn't be playing this game.*
>
> — KRIS BRYANT —

Kris Bryant worked hard during the offseason and spring to refine his swing so he could cut down on his strikeout rate in 2016.

The Cubs averaged more than 15,000 fans per game at Sloan Park in 2016, setting a new Cactus League attendance record.

FIRST HALF

THE CUBS JUMP OUT TO A BIG
LEAD AND NEVER LOOK BACK

There's an old saying in sports: It's not how you start; it's how you finish. But it would be short-sighted to apply that axiom to the Cubs' season. Though the players hefted the Commissioner's Trophy in early November, the lift they gave themselves at the season's outset was a large reason they finished the regular season with the best record in baseball, at 103-58, and an extremely comfortable 17.5-game lead in the NL Central.

Though the burden of entering the regular season as the World Series favorites could have hamstrung a young team, the Cubs managed to sprint out to a fast April start, dominating the competition to the tune of a 17-5 record and a +79 run differential. April 8 was the final day of the 2016 season they would spend out of first place in the division.

But the news wasn't all positive. In just the third game of the campaign, the Cubs lost catcher/outfielder Kyle Schwarber in dramatic fashion when he collided with center fielder Dexter Fowler while trying to make a play in Arizona. The young slugger tore the ACL and LCL in his left knee and was expected to be out for the season.

"The most important things to Kyle at this point are winning and staying connected to the team," said Cubs President of Baseball Operations Theo Epstein. "Everyone who knows Kyle was sick watching that play and the aftermath of that play. Just devastated for him. It's tough news. It's really devastating news, but we have to follow his example. In the wake of this injury, he's putting the team first."

Still, the Cubs got the home slate off to a good start against the Reds on April 11. The team entered the bottom of the eighth inning down 3-2, but Addison Russell delivered a clutch three-run homer off reliever Jumbo Diaz to give his team all the cushion it would need.

The most dominant individual effort of the month occurred on April 21 in Cincinnati, when Jake Arrieta, still basking in the afterglow of his 2015 Cy Young Award, dismantled the Reds with a six-strikeout no-hitter. The hirsute right-hander threw 119 pitches on the night, while the offense propelled the club to a 16-0 win. It was the second no-hitter of Arrieta's career and his second in just 10 regular-season starts.

"It feels different the second time," Arrieta said. "I was a little more relaxed as the game progressed. Based on the way I threw the ball before the game started, I anticipated having to grind through some at-bats and some innings a little more than I did. You put it all together and have conviction with what you're throwing out there, and good things can happen."

Though the evening belonged to Arrieta, it also marked the first time backup catcher David Ross had ever caught a no-hitter in his 15-year career. During the postgame press conference, Arrieta made sure the well-respected receiver got just as much attention as he did. The humble Ross, however, tried to keep the conversation focused on the big right-hander.

"This is why he won the Cy Young last year," Ross said. "He's got the capability of doing that every night. I think mentally he expects to do that. He's not shocked when he does stuff like that."

Javier Baez celebrated Mother's Day in fine fashion at Wrigley Field on May 8, launching a walk-off home run in the 13th inning to cap a four-game sweep of the NL East-leading Nationals. With the Cubs trailing 3-1 in the seventh inning, reliever Trevor Cahill led off with a single and later scored on Kris Bryant's two-run single. The game stood deadlocked at 3-3 until the fourth frame of extras when Baez ripped a 2-2 pitch from reliever Blake Treinen deep into the left-center field bleachers to give the Cubs a come-from-behind victory.

"I was just trying to get on base and get a good pitch to hit," Baez said. "He is throwing hard, 97 with sink. After the second strike, I just sat on the slider because they have been throwing it to me this series a lot. I was just looking for that pitch."

The game also included a unique stat. Courtesy of Maddon's orders, reigning NL MVP Bryce Harper didn't record an official at-bat, despite

seven plate appearances. He was walked six times, as well as hit by a pitch.

In a sport in which playing 10 games over .500 generally merits a playoff berth, the Cubs didn't lose back-to-back contests until they dropped both ends of a May 11 doubleheader against San Diego, in games 32 and 33 of the season.

On June 27, Bryant broke out of a mini-slump in a big way. The young slugger made history when he homered three times and doubled twice in a thrilling 11-8 Cubs win in Cincinnati. Remarkably, it was the first time in baseball history a player finished with that stat line. He was also the youngest Cub ever to homer three times in a game and the first to do so since Dioner Navarro in 2013.

"The last couple of weeks haven't been what I've wanted, so I figured I'm due," Bryant said after the game. "I'll remember this one for a long time."

The following night, fans were treated to a showcase of Maddon's managerial creativity, as he pulled out all the stops to get his club a win in a marathon 15-inning affair at Great American Ball Park. As the contest moved into the 13th inning, every position player on the roster had been used. That's when things got really interesting.

Athletic left-handed pitcher Travis Wood came in as the left fielder in the bottom of the 13th. After the Cubs failed to score in

Wrigley Field gets set to host its home opener against the Reds on April 11.

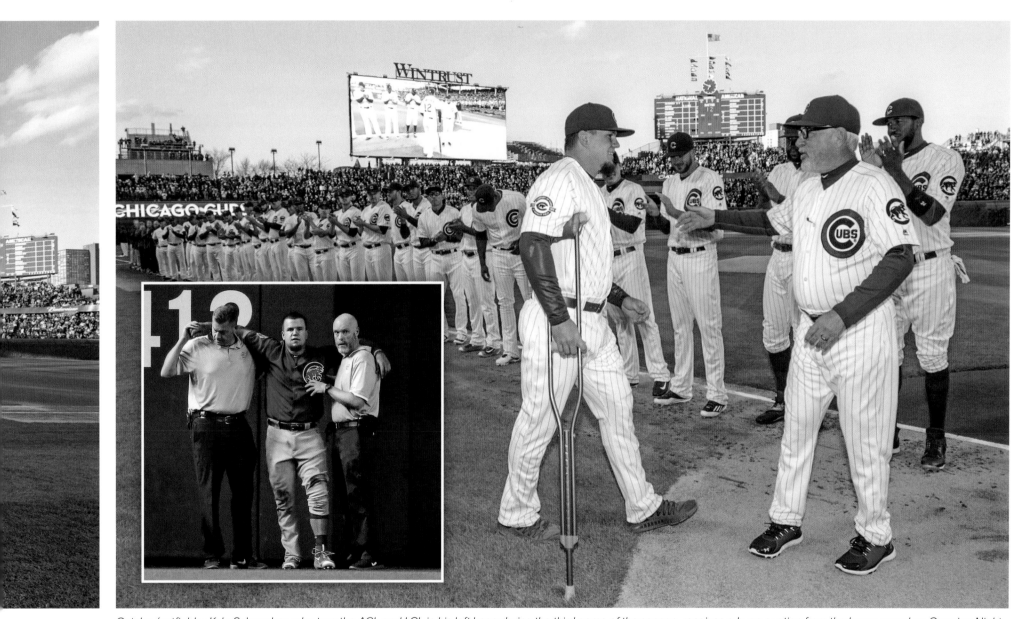

Catcher/outfielder Kyle Schwarber, who tore the ACL and LCL in his left knee during the third game of the season, receives a huge ovation from the home crowd on Opening Night.

The Cubs unveiled their spectacular new 30,000-square-foot clubhouse space in 2016. Over the last several years, the Cubs business operations team has upgraded facilities in the Dominican Republic, Arizona and Chicago.

the top of the 14th, Spencer Patton relieved Joel Peralta on the mound. The righty Patton induced right-handed hitter Brandon Phillips to fly out. Patton then moved to left field in a straight switch with Wood, who came to the mound to face lefty Jay Bruce. After getting Bruce to ground out, Wood went back to left field, and Patton returned to the mound to handle righty Adam Duvall, who also grounded out.

Bryant drove in a run in the top of the 15th before Baez hit a grand slam to put the Cubs up 7-2. In the bottom of the frame, Wood moved back from left field to pitcher, and reliever Pedro Strop slotted into left field, technically replacing Jason Hammel, who had pinch-hit for Patton in the top of the inning. Strop would finish the game in left field. It was the first time any of the three had played a position other than pitcher in their big-league careers.

"It was a lot of fun," Wood said. "I would have liked to have recorded an out and showcase some talents out there because I've tried to get Joe to put me out there and get me a couple starts."

Although the Cubs stumbled heading into the All-Star break during a grueling stretch in which they played games in 24 straight days, they still finished the first half with a 53-35 record, the NL Central lead and the second-best mark in the NL. ◑

The 2016 season marked Len Kasper's 12th year as the television voice of the Cubs and Jim Deshaies' fourth as an analyst.

Jake Arrieta and David Ross celebrate the right-hander's second career no-hitter, on April 21, a 16-0 romp in Cincinnati.

Javier Baez celebrates his Mother's Day walk-off homer in the bottom of the 13th inning to give the Cubs a 4-3 win over the Nationals on May 8.

David Ross and Anthony Rizzo douse Javier Baez with water after he hit a game-winning home run in the 13th inning on May 8.

Clark the Cub celebrates Jake Arrieta's 2015 no-hitter at Wrigley Field.

Free-agent signee John Lackey pitched 6.2 scoreless innings in a 6-0 win against Arizona on June 3. He went 7-5 with a 3.70 ERA in the season's first half.

> "Over time, I think [the new clubhouse] will absolutely be a benefit to our guys, keep them healthier, help them get prepared, get them in great form. Guys are showing up earlier now to take advantage of the facilities, so it's a great thing."
>
> — THEO EPSTEIN —

Addison Russell makes a diving backhanded grab against Pittsburgh on May 15. The Cubs had baseball's top-ranked defense in 2016.

The Cubs' new clubhouse space features historical memorabilia from important players and moments in franchise history.

On June 27, Kris Bryant became the first player ever to go 5-for-5 with three home runs and two doubles, in an 11-8 Cubs win in Cincinnati.

Dexter Fowler personified the "You go, we go" philosophy in 2016, driving the Cubs offense.

"I envisioned pitching like this, even when I had a 5.00 [ERA] in Baltimore. I expected to get to this point. Regardless of how long it took or what I had to go through to get there, I had visualizations of throwing no-hitters or throwing shutouts."

— JAKE ARRIETA —

Willson Contreras gets a curtain call after homering on the first pitch of his big-league career on June 19.

Ben Zobrist's professionalism on both sides of the ball were on display all season long.

Matt Szczur's eighth-inning grand slam puts an April 29 game against the Braves out of reach.

David Ross pours water over Matt Szczur following the outfielder's first career grand slam on April 29.

The Cubs prepare to board the bus for a 10-game road trip in early May. The "minimalist zany suit" trip was the first themed trip of 2016.

Javier Baez became one of the most valuable utilitymen in the game in 2016, proving to be an elite defensive player and a fan favorite.

Anthony Rizzo applies the tag at first to nab the Nationals' Anthony Rendon on a David Ross pickoff on May 6.

Gold Glover Jason Heyward slides to make a catch on May 1 against Atlanta, his former team.

Hector Rondon posted a 1.72 ERA and 42 strikeouts in 31.1 first-half innings as the Cubs closer.

Hall of Famers Billy Williams, Ryne Sandberg and Fergie Jenkins take the field before a July 6 game against Cincinnati.

Jake Arrieta followed up his 2015 Cy Young Award by going 12-4 with a 2.68 ERA in 18 first-half starts.

Pedro Strop, Javier Baez, Hector Rondon, traveling secretary Vijay Tekchandani and Matt Szczur show off their custom Cubs track suits for a nine-game road trip in early June.

Catalyst Anthony Rizzo was a consistent force in the Cubs' three hole throughout 2016.

Javier Baez rounds the bases after a third-inning home run on July 5.

Ever since I hit 99 [home runs], all I hear is, 'Hit a homer, grandpa.' Nobody knows my first name anymore.

— DAVID ROSS —

Justin Grimm appeared in 68 games in 2016, posting a 4.10 ERA with 11.1 K/9.

David Ross tips his cap to fans following his 100th career home run, which came on May 27 versus Philadelphia.

Addison Russell progressed into an All-Star shortstop in 2016.

Every time we come [to Wrigley Field], it's just such a treat. Honestly, everybody feels that way, all the guys. We want to hang out here pretty much all day. It's hard to get us to leave.

— KYLE HENDRICKS —

By mid-June, the ivy covering the brick walls in the Wrigley Field outfield was in full bloom.

ALL-STAR GAME

THE CUBS SEND SEVEN PLAYERS
TO THE MIDSUMMER CLASSIC

In some ways, the 2016 Cubs were a near-perfect storm from a fan perspective. Mix in a storied franchise, a major media market, first-place baseball, and a group of appealing and hard-working players, and there were plenty of reasons so many eyes were on the North Side this season.

So when the Chicago squad entered July with a comfortable lead in one of the toughest divisions in baseball, it wasn't so much a debate about which Cubs players would make the All-Star team in San Diego, but about just how many.

The final tally was impressive, as the National League roster featured seven players wearing Cubbie blue, including the entire starting infield—Kris Bryant, Anthony Rizzo, Addison Russell and Ben Zobrist—via the fan vote. The 2016 Cubs became the first team to accomplish that feat since the 1963 Cardinals.

Despite a field full of superstars, Rizzo received the most All-Star votes of any major-league player, thanks to his .299 av-erage, 1.006 OPS and 21 homers in the first half. It was the young first baseman's third consecutive Midsummer Classic as a Cub.

"It's unreal," Rizzo said. "I'm very appre-ciative of [the fans' support]. I try to go out every day and play the game hard and the way it's supposed to be played."

Zobrist, also making his third trip to the All-Star Game, claimed the second base spot by a mere 88 votes over the Nationals' Daniel Murphy. The do-everything utility-man was a reliable force in the Cubs order, reaching base at a .388 clip with 13 homers and 17 doubles heading into the game. Bry-ant, 24, one of the young faces of the sport, made his second All-Star trip in as many campaigns. The reigning Rookie of the Year pulled into San Diego with 25 homers and a .962 OPS. Russell, making his All-Star debut at just 22 years old, got the nod at short for his spectacular defensive play and clutch hitting, which led to 51 first-half RBI.

"I think what that says is we have an incredible fan base that's in our corner," said Zobrist, a first-year Cub. "As players, we become the benefactors. ... We're glad we're Chicago Cubs now, and I think that's why a lot of players want to play for the Cubs."

Joining the infielders were staff ace Jon Lester, right-hander Jake Arrieta and outfielder Dexter Fowler. The latter two did not participate in the game because Arrieta had pitched just a few days prior, and Fowler was on the DL with a hamstring injury. The Cubs' seven All-Stars were the organization's largest contingent since the 2008 club sent eight to the showcase.

"What it does for your own personal self-esteem is very valu-able," said manager Joe Maddon. "There's fan acceptance within that. There's peer acceptance ... in the game you wanted to play since you were a kid. You're an All-Star. That's pretty sweet stuff."

Although the Senior Circuit was on the losing end of the 4-2 affair, surrendering home-field advantage in the World Series to the eventual American League champion—and later creating more DH at-bats for Kyle Schwarber—Cubs players still made an impact in San Diego. Bryant got the scoring started in the top of the first inning, driving a home run to left-center field on the first pitch he saw from White Sox ace Chris Sale. In the fourth inning, Rizzo singled to right off the Blue Jays' Aaron Sanchez. On the mound, Lester worked out of a jam to record the first two outs of the seventh inning. ◖

Ben Zobrist, Addison Russell, Dexter Fowler, Kris Bryant, Jake Arrieta, Jon Lester and Anthony Rizzo are honored at Wrigley Field.

Seven Cubs players enjoyed the brief midsummer vacation in San Diego. That was the team's largest All-Star contingent since sending eight players in 2008.

FLY THE W

The 2016 Cubs joined the 1963 Cardinals as the only teams to start their entire infield in the All-Star Game.

Kris Bryant gets the scoring started for the National League with a first-inning solo home run off White Sox ace Chris Sale.

Second baseman Ben Zobrist tracks down a Jose Altuve pop-up in the bottom of the first inning.

SECOND HALF

THE STREAKING CUBS RUN AWAY
WITH THE NL CENTRAL DIVISION

If the first half of the 2016 season was about setting the tone, the second half was about proving just how dominant this Cubs squad really was.

The All-Star break allowed the organization to flex its muscles with its heavy representation in San Diego, but it also gave the players a chance to actually relax their muscles. This appeared to be exactly what the Cubs needed, as their late-first-half slide became a distant memory with some strong play out of the gate.

The team opened up the back half of the campaign against two postseason contenders, the Rangers and the Mets, and came away with a 4-2 record and series victories in each matchup. Though these games were a modest sample size, they were an affirmation that the Cubs were back to their winning ways. The club won or split each of its next 10 series, including an 11-game winning streak from the end of July into mid-August. They would finish August 22-6, the franchise's most wins in a month since September 1945. That run put the squad an almost insurmountable 15 games up in the NL Central standings. During a stellar 35-game stretch that included parts of late July, all of August and early September, the Cubs won 28 games.

One of those wins was a thriller at Wrigley Field on July 31 against Seattle that was a prime example of how the club never quit until the final out. After a shaky Brian Matusz spot start, the Cubs found themselves in a 6-0 hole after three innings. The home team scored two runs in the fifth on a walk and a subsequent hit-by-pitch. Reliever Travis Wood came in for the top of the sixth inning and then hit for himself in the bottom of the frame. Manager Joe Maddon, not wanting to remove his lefty specialist, substituted Pedro Strop for Chris Coghlan in left field in the top part of the next inning and then swapped Wood and Strop, putting the southpaw in the outfield for the second time in 2016.

This time, Wood actually saw action, as Franklin Gutierrez hit a fly ball to deep left field, forcing the veteran pitcher into the ivy to make a highlight-reel grab. A Ben Zobrist RBI triple in the seventh made it 6-3. In the top of the eighth, Wood stayed in left for the first three batters of the inning. Strop was then replaced by outfielder Matt Szczur, who went to left as Wood came back in to pitch against lefty Leonys Martin. But Wood made things simple, getting out of the inning with a nice pickoff play.

In the bottom of the ninth, the Cubs managed to capitalize on some poor Mariners pitching to score three runs and tie the game. After two more scoreless innings, Jason Heyward led off the 12th with a double and then advanced to third on a fly out. Jon Lester, who had seven career hits up to that point, was called on to pinch-hit. The unlikeliest of offensive heroes dropped down a perfect squeeze bunt to drive in Heyward and give the Cubs a dramatic comeback win.

"I blacked out," Lester joked. "I wasn't thinking at all. There was no thinking for me. I was trying to pay attention and not miss any signs. I was just trying not to screw anything up."

On Sept. 4, Heyward again came up big in front of a raucous home crowd. The Cubs were hosting San Francisco during a pivotal stretch during which they saw the Dodgers, Pirates and Giants in consecutive series. Trailing 2-1 in the bottom of the ninth, the Cubs were struggling to scrape together any hits. But Addison Russell doubled to lead off the inning and then advanced to third on a wild pitch. Heyward, who admittedly struggled with the bat in 2016, singled up the middle to tie the game. He stepped to the plate again to deliver the decisive blow in the 13th, driving a game-winning single into center field to plate Anthony Rizzo from second.

Kyle Hendricks took the mound on Sept. 12 and enjoyed arguably the most dominant outing of his career up to that point. Facing the rival Cardinals in St. Louis, the quiet right-hander dazzled his opponents, giving up zero hits over his first eight innings of work. Up 4-0 in the bottom of the ninth, Cards outfielder Jeremy Hazelbaker spoiled the no-hit bid with a homer to right field. Maddon then pulled his young hurler, who received a nice ovation from the road crowd. Hendricks finished the day with eight innings, 96 pitches and seven strikeouts.

"It's a different form of dominance," Maddon said of his precision pitcher. "Everyone wants dominance to be pure force. Finesse can be dominant also when it's done properly, when it's done like he does it."

On Sept. 16, the Cubs woke up division champions, as the second-place Cardinals had dropped the decisive contest the previous night. Though the Cubs were planning on celebrating regardless of their game's outcome, Miguel Montero made sure they got to do it in style. Trailing 4-2 against the Brewers entering the ninth inning, rookie Willson Contreras doubled to get things started. Chris Coghlan backed that up with a single and advanced to second on an error. A few batters later, Russell singled to score Coghlan, which tied the game and forced extra innings. Closer Aroldis Chapman came in and struck out the side before Montero hit a homer to deep left field in the bottom of the 10th. As he neared home, Montero dove onto the plate before getting dogpiled by his teammates, commencing an afternoon of celebration.

"This team is marked by a very selfless, team-first attitude," said President of Baseball Operations Theo Epstein. "It was fitting to have lots of guys contribute. Not just the stars, but everyone contributed today in the comeback. Then the consummate team player, Miguel Montero, who has handled his up-and-down year so, so well, to walk us off and prompt the celebration, it was very apropos."

Essentially, the only thing left to determine at that point was whom the Cubs would face at Wrigley Field to open up the National League Division Series. ◐

Anthony Rizzo makes a diving catch during a Sept. 4 game against the Giants.

Kris Bryant singles off Texas southpaw Cole Hamels on July 17.

David Ross celebrates Willson Contreras' three-run home run on Aug. 12 versus St. Louis.

Ben Zobrist beats a throw home on Sept. 15.

The Cubs welcomed 3,232,420 fans to Wrigley Field during the 2016 regular season.

Anthony Rizzo squeezes in an impromptu workout before a game in St. Louis.

Pitcher Travis Wood makes a running catch in the left-field ivy in a 7-6 win over the Mariners on July 31. He played left field on three separate occasions in 2016.

Jon Lester gets mobbed by teammates after laying down a perfect squeeze bunt to beat the Mariners in 12 innings on July 31.

Anthony Rizzo climbs on top of the side wall at Wrigley Field and reaches into the stands to make a spectacular catch against the Brewers on Aug. 16.

David Ross became a fan favorite during his two seasons with the team.

Javier Baez's defense shined at multiple positions in 2016.

Jason Heyward and Ben Zobrist congratulate each other after a big play against the Mets on July 20.

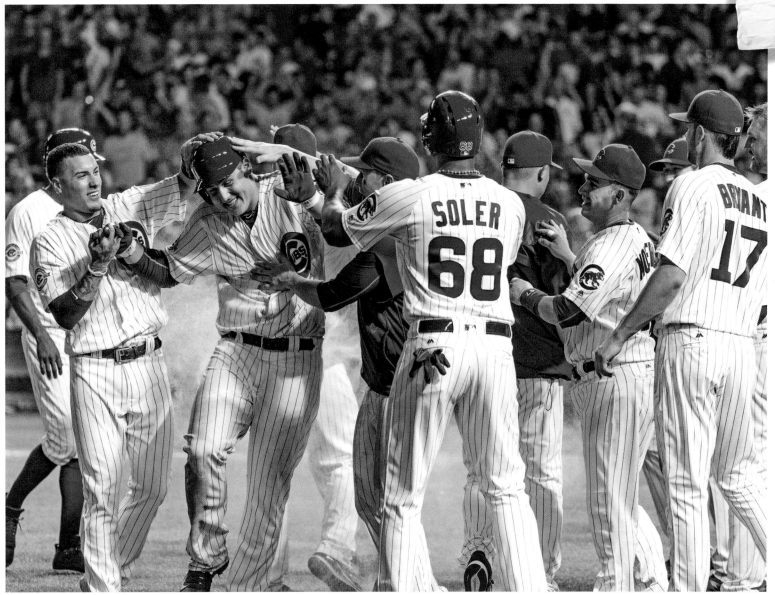

> "It's a lot of fun to be a Cub right now and go to that stadium and feel that energy."
>
> — DAVID ROSS —

Teammates mob Anthony Rizzo after his walk-off walk in the 11th inning against St. Louis on Aug. 11.

Ben Zobrist makes the turn at second against the Giants on Sept. 4.

Matt Szczur slides safely into home, scoring one of his four runs in a win against St. Louis on Aug. 12.

Javier Baez rounds third base in a 7-0 win against the Cardinals on Sept. 14.

Jason Heyward walks off the field after recording a game-winning hit against San Francisco on Sept. 4.

> "We just have fun. We're young. We just have a good time on the field and goofing around in the locker room."
>
> — KRIS BRYANT —

Veteran David Ross built a strong, big brother-type relationship with franchise faces Kris Bryant and Anthony Rizzo.

Kyle Hendricks salutes the fans after exiting a one-hit effort with no outs in the ninth inning in St. Louis on Sept. 12.

Right-hander Carl Edwards Jr. stepped into increasingly bigger bullpen roles as the season progressed.

There was no hiding Willson Contreras' passion for the game following his midseason call-up.

Continuing his breakout season, Addison Russell tips his cap to the fans after hitting a grand slam against the White Sox on July 27.

Kris Bryant and Anthony Rizzo combined to produce 71 home runs for the Bryzzo Souvenir Company in 2016.

"To be this young and to be this good, that's the part that's different for me. That's the part that stands out. Everyone is saying how good we are, but I'm telling you, these guys are going to get better."

— JOE MADDON —

The best view in baseball. Looking down at Wrigley Field from the center-field scoreboard on Sept. 3.

Cancer survivor Anthony Rizzo spends a great deal of his time off the field working with young cancer patients.

Jon Lester continued to show why he's one of the most dominant pitchers in baseball in 2016.

David Ross acknowledges the fans following his Sept. 25 home run against St. Louis.

Joe Maddon enjoys his sixth postseason appearance in 11 full seasons as a major-league manager.

Miguel Montero nears home plate after hitting a walk-off home run on Sept. 16, the same day the Cubs officially clinched a playoff spot.

Javier Baez celebrates in the clubhouse after the Cubs clinched a playoff berth for the second year in a row.

The Cubs pose for a picture around the mound after locking up the 2016 NL Central Division title.

The Cubs came into the postseason as the prohibitive favorites, outpacing the rest of baseball by 8.5 games in the regular season. But to get through the first round of the playoffs, they needed to knock off a formidable opponent: the San Francisco Giants, World Series champions in 2010, 2012 and 2014. As the old saying goes: To be the best, you have to beat the best.

Cubs fans have understood all season long that Javier Baez is much more valuable than your average utilityman. It took all of one postseason game in the national spotlight to demonstrate that fact to the wider baseball audience.

Much of the early postseason was like a Baez highlight reel, and it got going early in the National League Division Series. Game 1 at Wrigley Field was the pitching duel everyone expected, with Cubs ace Jon Lester facing off against Giants right-hander and NL All-Star Game starter Johnny Cueto.

With the game deadlocked at 0-0 and the Cubs able to muster only a pair of hits through the first seven innings, Baez stepped to the plate. Despite recording a single earlier in the game, the second baseman admitted he was looking to bunt because Cueto's multiple release angles upset his timing. But with the Giants third baseman playing in, Baez opted for a more direct approach, took his usual full swing and launched a ball to left that challenged the strong gusts blowing in from the north. Seemingly caught in a tussle between the wind and the 107 mph exit velocity off the bat, the ball dropped flush into the bottom of the left-field basket, prompting the restless fans at Wrigley Field to burst into a stadium-shaking roar.

"I thought I hit it really good. I thought it was way farther than that," Baez said. "It barely went out, but … it was a big hit for us."

As it turned out, that was all the scoring the Cubs would need. Lester pitched brilliantly, striking out five, walking none and scattering five hits over eight innings. He ceded the mound to closer Aroldis Chapman, who locked down the ninth for a 1-0 win.

While Game 2 may have lacked the edge-of-your-seat drama of the Cubs' first postseason affair, the team and its fans mostly have the pitchers to thank for that.

The Cubs grabbed an early lead on a first-inning single by Ben Zobrist, but it was the men on the mound who would do the most damage. With a 1-0 lead in the second, starter Kyle Hendricks dumped a two-run, bases-loaded single into short-center field. Before the frame was over, the Cubs sent eight hitters to the plate, taking a 4-0 lead, and making it a quick night for opposing starter and former Cub Jeff Samardzija.

With the Cubs leading 4-2 in the top of the fourth, Hendricks was forced to exit the game after he was hit in the arm by an Angel Pagan comebacker. Southpaw Travis Wood relieved Hendricks, and then relieved the crowd. After working out of the inning on the mound, Wood, always a good hitter in his starting days, came to the plate in the bottom of the frame and took the first pitch he saw out to deep left-center field to give the Cubs a 5-2 lead.

"[It] just feels good to be able to contribute at the plate as well as on the mound," Wood said. "That's what the pitchers are out there to do, especially the starting pitchers. Kyle's two RBI trump my one. He did an outstanding job tonight."

It was the first home run by a reliever in a postseason game since the Giants' Rosy Ryan hit one in 1924. After Hendricks went down, five relievers combined to pitch 5.1 scoreless innings, preserving the win.

It was important for the club to get into San Francisco with a lead, as Giants ace and playoff hero Madison Bumgarner loomed in Game 3. The contest took a major turn in the Cubs' favor in the top of the second, however, when starting pitcher Jake Arrieta deposited a 1-2 fastball into the left-field stands for a three-run homer. The 2015 Cy Young winner exited the game with a 3-2 lead after retiring the side in order in the sixth. In the bottom of the eighth, unlikely Giants hero Conor Gillaspie put his club in front with a two-run triple, and Brandon Crawford drove Gillaspie in a batter later with a single.

But the Cubs were far from done. With his club trailing by two runs in the top of the ninth inning, Dexter Fowler worked a leadoff

walk, and Kris Bryant backed him up with a home run that just left the yard to tie it up. Even though Bryant called it the biggest homer of his career, it would ultimately go for naught.

With the bullpen stretched thin, reliever Mike Montgomery turned in a yeoman's effort. The left-hander gave up just two hits from the ninth inning through the top of the 13th, when he surrendered back-to-back doubles, including Joe Panik's game winner, to cut the Cubs' series lead to 2-1.

Game 4 of the NLDS didn't really heat up until the ninth inning. To that point, Giants starter Matt Moore had limited Cubs batters to just two hits, though one was a David Ross homer in the third. With Chicago trailing 5-2 entering the final frame of regulation, win probability charts gave the team a 3 percent chance of coming away victorious. But Bryant singled to left, and first baseman Anthony Rizzo drew a walk. Zobrist then ripped a double down the right-field line, scoring Bryant and putting men on second and third with nobody out. That's when the chess match really began.

Manager Joe Maddon opted to play the matchups and pinch-hit Chris Coghlan for Addison Russell. To counter, Giants manager Bruce Bochy called on left-hander Will Smith. Maddon then subbed out Coghlan for rookie Willson Contreras, who promptly drove in both runs to tie the game on a single up the

Wayne Messmer delivers the national anthem prior to Game 1 of the NLDS at Wrigley Field.

Joe Maddon and Billy Williams keep things loose before Game 1 gets underway.

Jorge Soler joins bullpen stalwarts Pedro Strop, Hector Rondon and Aroldis Chapman prior to Game 1.

middle. Jason Heyward forced Contreras out at second, but got to second himself on a rare throwing error by shortstop Brandon Crawford. This set up Baez to complete the epic comeback with a hard single up the middle that scored Heyward and gave the Cubs a 6-5 lead they wouldn't relinquish. It marked just the second time in playoff history a team came back from at least three runs down in the ninth inning of a series-clinching game.

"There's 27 outs, and you don't give any of them up, and you keep playing for all 27," Maddon said. "After the game, even on the mound there taking the photographs, the guys were chanting, 'We don't quit, we don't quit.'

"We don't quit. That's really what it comes down to. You hear that all the time—everybody says it—but you have to actually live it. And I have to tell you, I've seen it so many times from this group. That's a big part of our philosophy. I like to keep things simple, and that's simple. I don't want to get complicated. We just play 27 outs."

The win snapped the Giants' remarkable streak of 10 consecutive postseason series wins. It was also the first even calendar year since 2008 San Francisco didn't finish as World Series champs.

With the NLDS in their back pocket, the Cubs headed back to Wrigley Field for an NLCS confrontation with the NL West champion Los Angeles Dodgers. ◗

Albert Almora Jr. gets pumped up as he heads out onto the field prior to Game 1.

Javier Baez applies a tag to Conor Gillaspie after David Ross threw behind the runner during Game 1.

Javier Baez watches his homer leave the yard during Game 1 of the NLDS. It was the lone run of the game.

Aroldis Chapman gave up one hit, but locked down the ninth to secure the Game 1 victory.

Scoreboard operator Fred Washington watches Game 1 from his usual spot. Washington started with the Cubs grounds crew in 1984 and retired after the 2016 season.

Hector Rondon soaks Javier Baez in the Cubs celebration room after the team's Game 1 victory.

Javier Baez points to
the sky after hitting a
homer to give the Cubs
a 1-0 lead in Game 1.

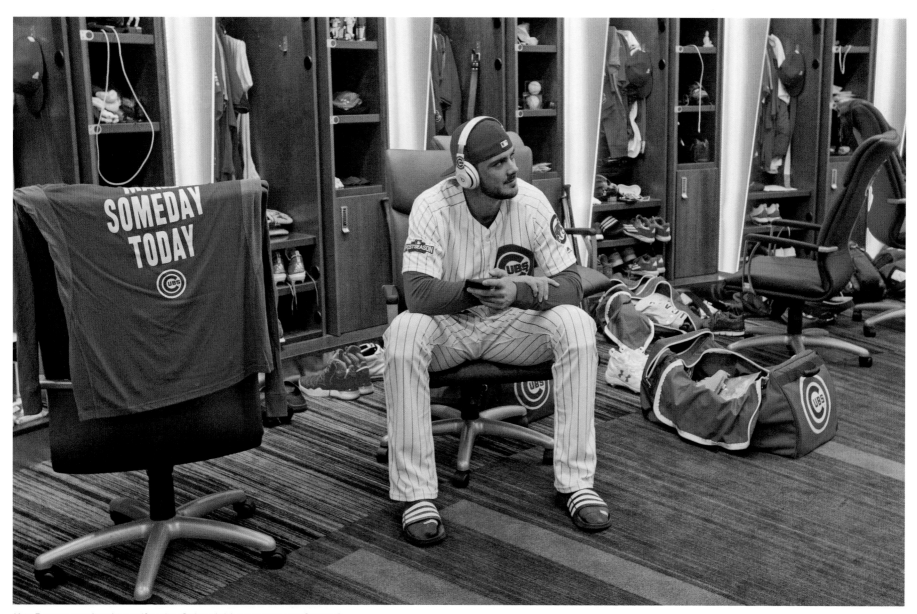

Kris Bryant readies himself in the Cubs clubhouse prior to Game 2.

  FLY THE W

First base coach Brandon Hyde gives Travis Wood a high five as Wood rounds the bases following his home run.

Ben Zobrist singles to drive in the first run of Game 2 versus San Francisco.

> "We wanted to make [Giants Game 2 starter Jeff Samardzija] throw strikes and make him put the ball in the zone, and that's what happened."
>
> — DEXTER FOWLER —

Rookie catcher Willson Contreras picked up two hits in Game 2 of the NLDS.

> *"I love the responsibility. I love that it falls on my shoulders. I love my job. The pressure is on, but I can handle that pressure. I understand the city and the fans are hyped, but I love that."*
>
> — AROLDIS CHAPMAN —

Aroldis Chapman fires a scoreless ninth inning to pick up his second save of the postseason.

Javier Baez celebrates his second-inning run.

Javier Baez slides safely into home after a Kyle Hendricks single during the second inning of Game 2.

The Giants and Cubs line up for the national anthem prior to Game 3 in San Francisco.

> "I just wanted to put a nice, easy swing on it and try and find the barrel. That's what I was able to do. It put us in a good spot. We had a chance to win the game, but they made some plays and swung the bat really well to turn the tides in their favor."
>
> — JAKE ARRIETA —

Jake Arrieta watches his second-inning home run clear the fence during Game 3.

Jake Arrieta's blast gave the Cubs an early 3-0 lead.

Javier Baez and Pedro Strop joke around in the Cubs dugout during Game 3.

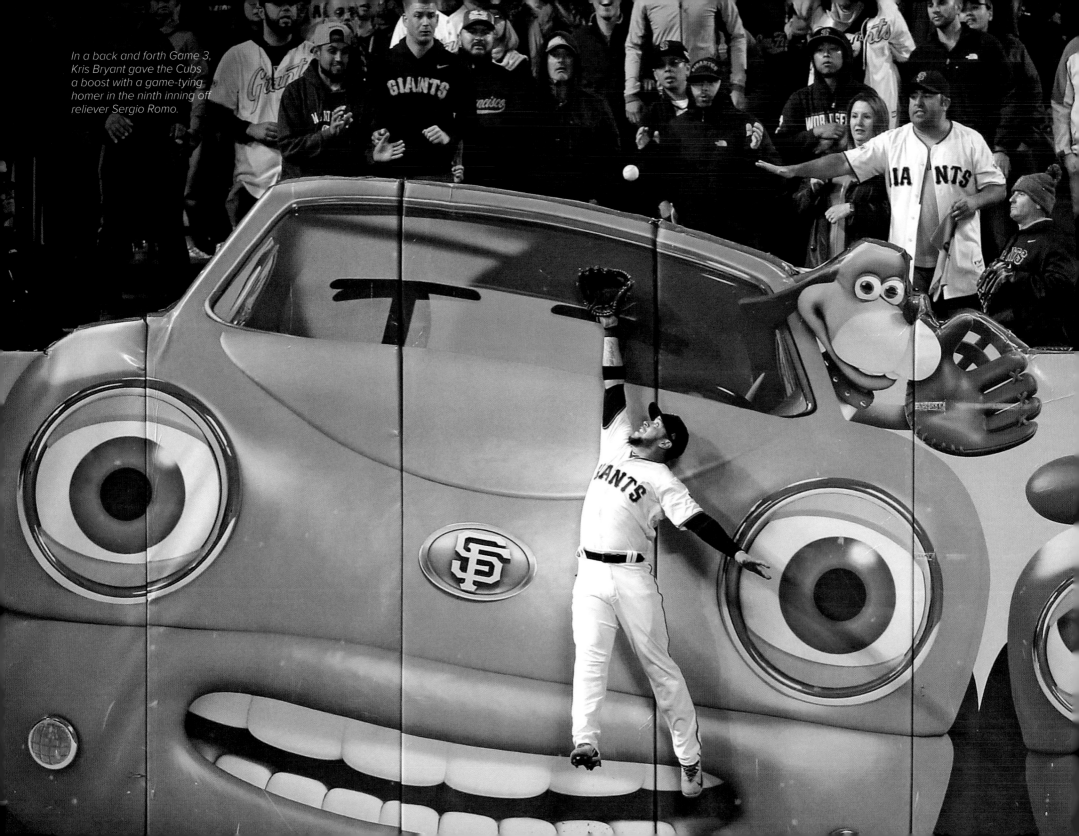

In a back and forth Game 3, Kris Bryant gave the Cubs a boost with a game-tying homer in the ninth inning off reliever Sergio Romo.

[Game 3] was fun to be a part of, even though we didn't win. We gave it all we've got. Great at-bats, one through nine, and from our pitchers too. It was just a great game."

— KRIS BRYANT —

Closer Aroldis Chapman hugs Kris Bryant after his ninth-inning, game-tying home run in Game 3.

John Lackey went four innings and gave up three runs during Game 4 against the Giants.

David Ross rips a third-inning home run to left field to tie things up in Game 4.

Teammates mob Jason Heyward after he scores the go-ahead run in Game 4. His run would seal the series, three games to one.

Javier Baez makes a throw from his knees in Game 4.

Teammates congratulate Anthony Rizzo after he scores a run during the big ninth-inning comeback in Game 4.

> "Hitting before the ninth inning is overrated anyway. It's about doing it when it matters, I guess."
> — THEO EPSTEIN —

Closer Aroldis Chapman celebrates recording the final out of the series.

The Cubs gather on the mound after eliminating the Giants and moving on to the NLCS.

The Cubs revel in their NLDS victory on the pitcher's mound in San Francisco.

Aroldis Chapman gets sprayed with Champagne following the Cubs' Game 4 win.

A soaking wet Joe Maddon sports a custom Cubs wetsuit for the postgame celebration.

Anthony Rizzo toasts the team following Game 4.

[We did it] in a really difficult environment against a team that hasn't lost a closeout game in a while. All that stuff matters. All that matters is that we continue to move forward and establish this identity as being a team that plays well in the postseason.

— JOE MADDON —

Chairman Tom Ricketts joins the team in the clubhouse after the Cubs' NLDS series victory.

NATIONAL LEAGUE
CHAMPIONSHIP SERIES

If the National League Championship Series matchup against the Dodgers demonstrated one thing about the 2016 Cubs, it was their remarkable ability to grind out games until the final out. That resiliency was on full display throughout a tense six-game series with the NL West champs.

The one advantage the Cubs had over Los Angeles was the ability to reset their rotation, a luxury they earned by winning the previous series in four games, versus the five it took the Dodgers to send the Nationals packing. On paper, Game 1 favored the Cubs, as ace Jon Lester matched up against struggling Dodgers starter Kenta Maeda. It took all of two batters for the Cubs to jump out in front, as leadoff man Dexter Fowler, in typical "you go, we go" fashion, singled and scored a batter later on a Kris Bryant double.

Javier Baez picked up where he left off in the NLDS, driving in the second run of the game in the second inning. His star shined even brighter after he stole home a few batters later when catcher Carlos Ruiz attempted to back-pick him at third.

The Cubs continued to cruise, even after Lester gave up a wind-aided homer to Andre Ethier in the fifth inning. The lefty would go six innings, surrendering just one run on four hits. The game remained strongly in the Cubs' favor, until Dodgers first baseman Adrian Gonzalez tied things up 3-3 with a two-run single in the eighth.

But the Cubs were undaunted. Ben Zobrist opened up the bottom of the eighth with a double, before Addison Russell grounded out. Dodgers manager Dave Roberts then elected to intentionally walk Jason Heyward and later Chris Coghlan to load the bases for pinch-hitter Miguel Montero. The backup catcher, who saw limited action in the postseason, made his opponents pay with a grand slam to right field, leaving the home crowd ecstatic.

"As a kid, you always dream of the situations, and that's what you live for," Montero said. "It's easy to hit a grand slam in the first inning when nobody is actually screaming at it. This one is a lot more special."

Fans were going so crazy, many missed Fowler's subsequent home run to right. The Dodgers got one back in the ninth, but the game ended 8-4, putting the Cubs up 1-0 in the series.

The next two games brought the club down from cloud nine. Dominant outings from Dodgers ace Clayton Kershaw and midseason acquisition Rich Hill turned a 1-0 series lead into a 2-1 deficit. The Cubs were limited to just six hits combined in the two shutout losses.

"I've got a lot of faith in our guys," said manager Joe Maddon after the Cubs traveled to Los Angeles. "It's a difficult moment to be in to come back out here on the first game here, two more left before we get to go home, and you have to fight through some pretty stringent adversity."

Winning a single inning is a minor victory in an extended postseason run, but it might be argued the fourth inning of Game 4 was the most important of the NLCS. In the first three games of the series, the Cubs were hitting just .164, but momentum swung after one key at-bat from a playoff-tested veteran.

Dodgers 20-year-old rookie Julio Urias had been cruising through the first three frames, but Zobrist changed things up by laying down a perfect leadoff bunt for a single in the fourth. After another single by Baez, Willson Contreras laced a liner to left, scoring Zobrist. Jason Heyward grounded out to bring in Baez. Then shortstop Russell, who had struggled throughout the postseason offensively, stepped to the dish and drove a 2-0 fastball into the right-center field stands to give the Cubs a 4-0 lead.

In the fifth inning, Anthony Rizzo—another potent member of the Cubs offense who had been cold up to that point—smashed a pitch off reliever Pedro Baez to deep right-center to give the Cubs a 5-0 lead. To jump-start his bat, Rizzo decided to try someone else's. The All-Star first baseman had opted for reserve outfielder Matt Szczur's lighter and shorter bat for the home run and continued to use it to great effect throughout the remainder of the

postseason. The Cubs would get another five runs in the sixth via a Fowler single, a two-run Rizzo single, a Baez sacrifice fly and an error. The game ultimately wrapped up 10-2 in the Cubs' favor.

"The work ethic and what you do is there. Our confidence is up," Rizzo said. "The best part about the postseason is it's the next at-bat. You've got to turn the page to the next at-bat, and you've got to be ready for that big situation."

Game 5 was a pivotal contest, as the Cubs were hoping to get back to Wrigley Field up in the series. By the end of the first inning, Rizzo's slump was officially an afterthought. With Fowler on first base, Rizzo ripped a double to score the leadoff man, putting the Cubs up 1-0. From there, they rode starter Lester, who mowed down opposing hitters, going seven strong innings, surrendering just one run and notching six strikeouts.

Russell continued his torrid pace, crushing a two-run bomb in the top of the sixth, and the team piled on from there, closing out a comfortable 8-4 win.

"Skip, that's all he wants is people on base, and we got people on base," Russell said. "Right there, that situation, just trying not to do too much. I was just trying to find some gaps. First pitch slider a little bit low. Second pitch was a slider, but it was elevated. I put the barrel on it, and it kind of went. But just rounding bases, it was pretty exciting. Pumped up. Not only for myself, but for the team and that little cushion that Jonny [Lester] had to go forward from that."

The view from the Wrigley Field scoreboard as the Cubs and Dodgers line up prior to Game 1 of the NLCS.

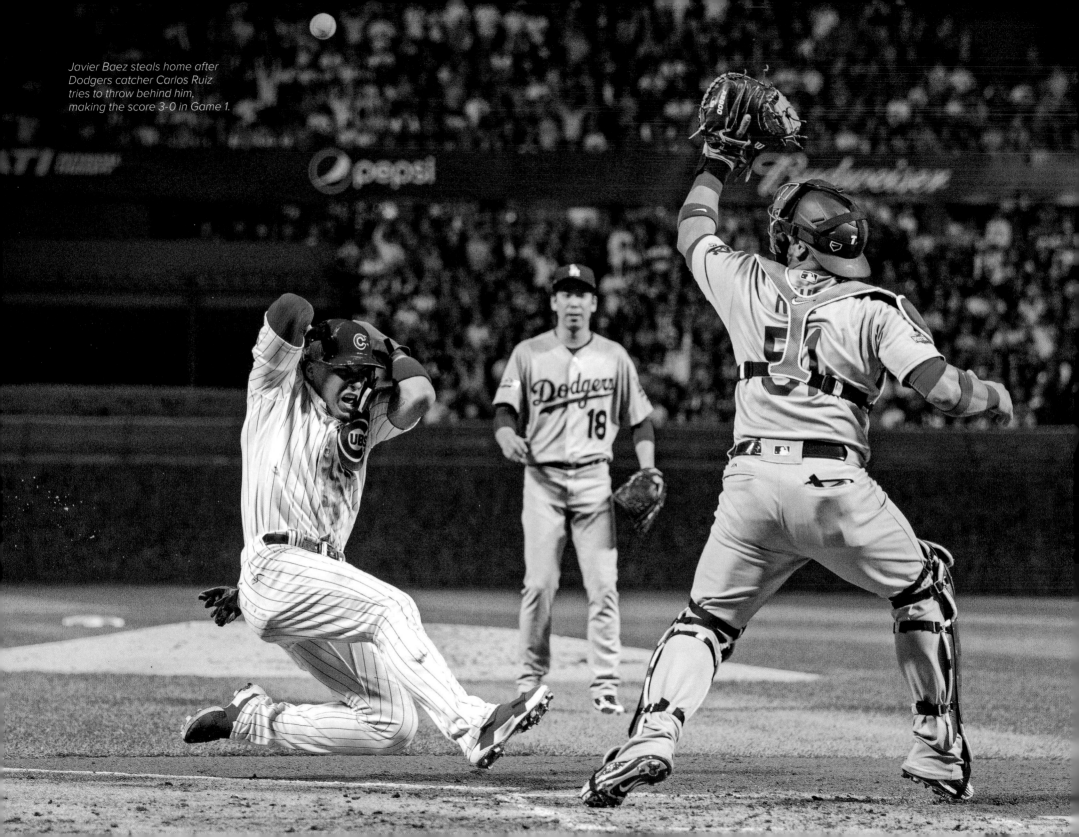

Javier Baez steals home after Dodgers catcher Carlos Ruiz tries to throw behind him, making the score 3-0 in Game 1.

Jason Heyward dives into third base after a second-inning triple.

That victory set the stage for perhaps the most anticipated game in Wrigley Field history, as the Cubs pulled into Chicago with a chance to close out the Dodgers and head to the World Series for the first time since 1945. The scene around the Friendly Confines was nothing short of controlled chaos. Thousands lined the streets, as bars and restaurants reached capacity long before first pitch. Even though the Cubs had a Cy Young finalist taking the mound in Kyle Hendricks, the Dodgers were throwing three-time Cy Young winner Kershaw.

For the second straight game, the Cubs didn't wait long to get the scoring started. Fowler led off with a ground-rule double in the first, and Bryant singled to right, sending fans all over the country into hysterics. After Bryant moved to third on a fielding error by left fielder Andrew Toles, Zobrist hit a sacrifice fly to make it 2-0.

That was more support than Hendricks would need. The right-hander, in perhaps the best outing of his breakout season, gave up a leadoff single to start the game, but managed to face the minimum until he was pulled with one out in the eighth. The Cubs ran Kershaw out of the game after the fifth, tacking on three more runs. After Hendricks departed, closer Aroldis Chapman shut the door with a five-out save, giving the Cubs a 5-0 win and the National League pennant.

Players celebrated in the clubhouse before moving to a temporary podium set up on the edge of the outfield grass. Baez and Lester were awarded NLCS co-MVPs in front of a fully packed stadium of fans who remained in the ballpark to witness history. ◐

"We don't quit. That's what the boys yell all the time. It's something that you have to nurture. Better teams have that. You have to have that in order to win as many games as we did."

— JOE MADDON —

Jon Lester applauds the efforts of Dexter Fowler. All season long, the Cubs had the top-ranked defense in baseball.

Dexter Fowler lays out to make a backhanded catch in center field to rob the Dodgers of a hit during the first game of the NLCS.

A half inning after the Dodgers tied the score in the eighth, pinch-hitter Miguel Montero smacks a grand slam to right to put Game 1 out of reach.

Miguel Montero tips his cap to the fans following his dramatic eighth-inning grand slam in Game 1.

EMBRACE THE TARGET

THERE'S SUNSHINE, FRESH AIR, AND THE TEAM'S BEHIND US

DON'T LET THE PRESSURE EXCEED

CUBS

RUSSELL
27

Addison Russell heads to the field for Game 2 of the NLCS at Wrigley Field.

Dexter Fowler faces off against three-time Cy Young winner Clayton Kershaw in Game 2.

> "Tonight we hit some balls hard and hit some balls to the track, and they didn't fall. They hit one over the fence and that was it, 1-0."
>
> — JASON HEYWARD —

Addison Russell puts the tag on Adrian Gonzalez to complete a heads-up double play started by second baseman Javier Baez.

Cubs players get stretched out and enjoy the weather on the workout day before Game 3 in Los Angeles.

Addison Russell, who had been struggling in the NLCS, talks hitting with manager Joe Maddon.

> "It is a little bit concerning in the sense because we kind of got stuck [in the NLCS] last year. We got to this particular point and then ran into a hot pitching staff with the Mets. So that's part of why I wanted to manipulate the lineup a little bit today to see if we could unearth some things."
>
> — JOE MADDON —

The Cubs line up for player introductions prior to getting shut out by Rich Hill in Game 3 of the NLCS in Los Angeles.

Kris Bryant was one of the few offensive bright spots in Game 3, going 2-for-4 against Dodgers starter Rich Hill.

Game 4 starter John Lackey
went four innings and gave up
two runs in a 10-2 Cubs win.

Coaches congratulate
Willson Contreras after he
tagged out Adrian Gonzalez
at home in Game 4.

Ben Zobrist gets things going in the
fourth inning of Game 4 with a key
leadoff bunt against Los Angeles.

Willson Contreras celebrates Addison Russell's fourth-inning home run during Game 4.

The Cubs dugout reacts to Addison Russell's homer.

Addison Russell hits a two-run bomb during Game 4 to give the Cubs a 4-0 lead.

Joe Maddon leads his troops in the visitors' dugout during Game 4.

Joe Maddon talks with Dexter Fowler on the dugout railing.

> "We have a lot of talent on this team, but we have a lot of guys that are dirt-ballers that get down and get dirty and make a lot of plays and have some dirty at-bats for us too."
>
> — JON LESTER —

Bench coach Dave Martinez and Kris Bryant share a laugh in the dugout.

Jon Lester was dominant in Game 5, going seven innings and giving up one run on five hits.

David Ross records a double off Dodgers reliever Joe Blanton in the sixth inning of Game 5.

Anthony Rizzo hit .320 in the NLCS against the Dodgers with two home runs and five RBI.

Cubs fans gather outside of the Wrigley Field Budweiser Bleachers during Game 6 of the NLCS.

"There's angst. There's all that kind of good stuff. It's just a fan base that's been waiting for a while. We're definitely on the verge of doing something wonderful, and they're absolutely engaged and involved."

— JOE MADDON —

Kerry Wood throws out the first pitch before Game 6 in a Ron Santo jersey.

Cubs pitcher Kyle Hendricks picks off Dodgers outfielder Josh Reddick in the second inning of Game 6.

Javier Baez makes a catch in front of teammate Anthony Rizzo in the fifth inning of Game 6.

Addison Russell revs the engine after his second-inning double.

Kyle Hendricks was brilliant in the Game 6 win, going 7.1 innings, striking out six and giving up only two hits.

Anthony Rizzo watches his fifth-inning home run leave the Friendly Confines in Game 6.

Anthony Rizzo marks the final out, as the Cubs clinch the National League pennant for the first time since 1945.

The Cubs infield celebrates history at Wrigley Field before moving on to face the Cleveland Indians in the World Series.

Fred Washington raises the W flag at Wrigley Field after the Game 6 win. The Cubs have been flying the W after victories since 1937.

Cubs Chairman Tom Ricketts hoists the National League Championship Trophy with President of Baseball Operations Theo Epstein.

The Cubs baseball operations department enjoys the moment on the mound following Game 6.

Cubs fans snap photos of the marquee as the Cubs head to the World Series.

Champagne flows in the clubhouse, following the Cubs' 4-2 series win over the Dodgers in the NLCS.

Jon Lester and Javier Baez are named NLCS co-MVPs. Lester went 1-0 with a 1.38 ERA in the series, and Baez hit .318 and drove in five runs.

Fans mobbed the streets outside Wrigley Field following the Cubs' Game 6 win.

Jake Arrieta, David Ross and Dave Martinez celebrate on the field.

Joe Maddon gets a roar from the crowd following the Cubs' NLCS-clinching win.

Anthony Rizzo waves a Cubs flag on the field during the Cubs' celebration.

The Cubs celebrate their pennant-clinching victory around the pitcher's mound at Wrigley Field.

Dexter Fowler enjoys his moment in the Cubs' celebration room.

Miguel Montero is doused after the Cubs' series-clinching victory.

CUBS vs. INDIANS
WORLD SERIES

THE NEVER-SAY-DIE CUBS COMPLETE A COMEBACK FOR THE AGES

The most dramatic pursuit in professional sports concluded in appropriately dramatic fashion, as the Chicago Cubs Baseball Club looked to put its demons to rest and finally bring a long-awaited world championship to the North Side. The Cubs, most experts' preseason World Series favorite, faced off against the red-hot Cleveland Indians, who had gone 7-1 in the postseason and boasted home-field advantage thanks to the American League's All-Star Game win in July.

But the Cubs still looked like a mismatch for the Tribe, who had lost two key starters to injury during the regular season. To compensate and maximize the potential appearances for ace Corey Kluber, Indians manager Terry Francona decided to go with a three-man rotation. The benefit was obvious—he was able to throw his most dominant starter, Kluber, three times, but it also meant his staff would all be working on three days' rest throughout the series. The Cubs knew it was important to get early leads, as Cleveland had bullpen stalwarts

Brian Shaw, Andrew Miller and Cody Allen waiting to lock down the late innings.

The Cubs received a huge emotional boost heading into the Fall Classic when slugger Kyle Schwarber was added to the World Series roster. The hard-hitting catcher/outfielder had sustained a serious knee injury in the third game of the campaign and wasn't expected to be ready until spring training 2017. But after rehabilitating all season at Wrigley Field's new facilities and receiving a surprisingly positive medical evaluation during the NLCS, doctors cleared him to begin hitting and running. Though he couldn't play the outfield, he was available to DH during the four games at Progressive Field and pinch-hit.

"When I got the news that I was not going to be held back in any way, I called Theo [Epstein] right away, and I was like, 'Hey, I'd love the opportunity to try,'" Schwarber said. "Knowing that I had the opportunity to try and get back, it would kill me deep inside if I didn't. And I knew going into it there were no guarantees.

"I didn't do it for this reason. I didn't want the media attention. I didn't want any of that. I did it for my teammates. I did it for me too. That's the competitor in me. Like I said, those guys, that's a special clubhouse we've got, and that's why I did it."

It was a battle of aces as the Cubs pulled into Progressive Field, with lefty Jon Lester facing off against Cleveland righty Kluber, who had gone 18-9 with a 3.14 ERA in the regular season and been dominant in three postseason starts. Any thoughts of a series mismatch were immediately dispatched when Cleveland jumped on Lester for two first-inning runs. Kluber never looked back from there, spinning six scoreless innings with nine strikeouts, before turning over the last three frames to Miller and Allen. The Indians pulled away late for an easy 6-0 win.

The Cubs took care of business in Game 2 behind starter Jake Arrieta, who delivered five no-hit innings before allowing two hits in the sixth and giving way to Mike Montgomery and Aroldis Chapman. The Cubs jumped on the board early with a Kris Bryant single and an Anthony Rizzo double off starter Trevor Bauer in the first inning. But the big story on a cold Cleveland night was Schwarber, who went 2-for-4 and drove in two runs in the Cubs' 5-1 victory.

"He jacks everybody up," said Cubs manager Joe Maddon. "Those couple big hits he got, again, Rizzo really responded to it well. The whole group did. It makes your lineup longer. It makes it thicker. It makes it better. [Ben] Zobrist is seeing better pitches right now because of that too, I believe.

"So we knew what it would be like all year long. We didn't have it. And now we're going to have it in a short spurt right now, and it's kind of fun. It's a great weapon to have."

When the team headed back to Chicago with a series split, many fans were talking about finishing things off at Wrigley Field. But the Indians quickly shattered those fantasies, logging 1-0 and 7-2 wins in Games 3 and 4 before a shell-shocked home crowd.

With the Indians up 3-1 in the series and the final two games in Cleveland, the deck was stacked against the Cubs. It looked like the longest championship drought in American professional sports might extend for at least one more year. But as the Cubs liked to say all year, they never quit.

In a tense Game 5, with the team on the brink of elimination, the Indians jumped out to an early lead on a Jose Ramirez solo blast in the second inning. After being shut out for the first three frames, the Cubs got to starter Bauer in the fourth on a Bryant homer, a run-scoring single from Addison Russell and a sac fly from David Ross.

Lester was solid through six innings, and Carl Edwards Jr. came in to get the first out in the seventh. But with the season on the line, Maddon turned to Chapman for an unusual eight-out save. The Cubs escaped Chicago with a 3-2 victory in Game 5, giving the fans one last celebration at their home ballpark. And celebrate they did, shaking Wrigley Field with their cheers and streaming out into Wrigleyville to celebrate their team, come what may.

"Chappy coming in and doing what he's been doing for us since he came over here, and even before that, is pretty unbelievable to see," Lester said. "This guy is used to just getting three outs, and he goes what, 2.2 [innings]? That's a huge, huge uplift for our team. You know, he was fired up. We were all fired up to get through that against a good team—a good fastball-hitting team—regardless of how hard he throws."

The Cubs headed back to an unusually warm Progressive Field, where the temperature was in the mid-70s on Nov. 1, for Game 6. As the weather heated up, so too did the Cubs' bats. The offense jumped all over Indians starter Josh Tomlin and

Joe Maddon meets with the Fox broadcast crew in his office prior to Game 1 at Progressive Field.

Kyle Schwarber takes batting practice after being added to the World Series roster.

Jason Hammel relaxes before Game 1 by playing a little football.

reliever Dan Otero early, staking Arrieta to a 7-0 lead in the third inning on a Bryant solo shot and six RBI from Russell, who delivered a two-run double and a grand slam. His RBI total tied a World Series record. Bryant went 4-for-5 on the night, and Rizzo went 3-for-5.

"Being part of the Cubs, you're put in the limelight," Russell said. "Early on, you're forced to deliver whenever the game's kind of on the line. So having that practice throughout the whole season and then finally here comes the big moment in the postseason, in the World Series ... you definitely learn to control those feelings."

Though the Cubs had a 7-2 lead late, Maddon again called on Chapman to help close things out. After Rizzo smashed a two-run homer in the top of the ninth, the skipper got other bullpen arms moving, but Chapman still logged 1.1 innings.

In the end, the Cubs cruised to a comfortable 9-3 win, setting the stage for a dramatic Game 7 matchup against Kluber. Chicago fans packed Progressive Field to watch their club try to pull off a miraculous comeback, but Cleveland supporters were not to be outdone. The stadium was at concert-type decibel levels all game long as the momentum swung back and forth.

Dexter Fowler led off the game with a homer, and Kyle Hendricks looked sharp, despite some shaky defense behind him and a tight strike zone. The Indians tied the game up in the third on a Carlos Santana single, but by the top of the fifth, the

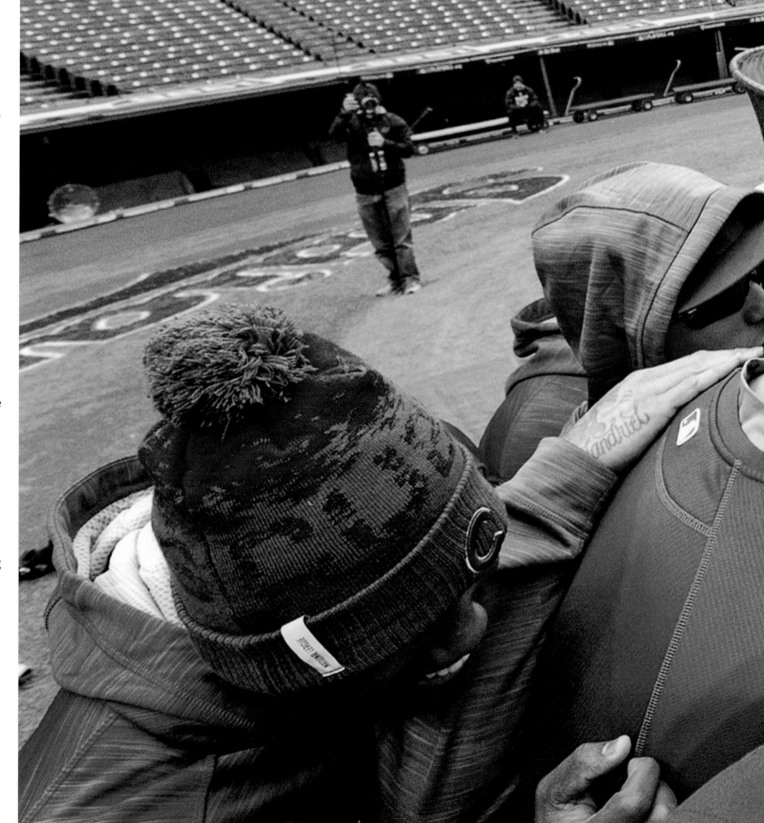

Prior to each playoff game, the team gathered on the field for a player meeting.

The Cubs and Indians line up for the national anthem before Game 1 at Progressive Field.

"There was an inordinate amount of expectations and pressure that was heaped upon us, and I tried to convince our guys that's a good thing. Why would you ever want to do anything or be part of a situation or moment that did not have great expectations?"

— JOE MADDON —

Joe Maddon talks to DH and No. 5 hitter Kyle Schwarber prior to Game 1 in Cleveland.

The Cubs enjoy player introductions before the World Series kicks off.

Cubs had built up a 5-1 lead on a Russell sac fly, a Willson Contreras double, a Javier Baez home run and a Rizzo single.

After Hendricks gave up a two-out walk in the bottom of the fifth, Maddon decided to bring in ace Lester, who had been warming in the 'pen. The left-hander gave up a quick single to Jason Kipnis and then unleashed a wild pitch that plated two Cleveland runs. Still, the Cubs moved into the eighth with a 6-3 lead, thanks to a Ross sixth-inning homer. When Lester gave way with two outs in the bottom of the eighth, Maddon again called on Chapman, but this time the flame-throwing lefty was running on fumes, with his trademark 103 mph fastball down to a more manageable 98.

In the bottom of the eighth, the Tribe got to Chapman for three runs, including a crucial game-tying, two-run homer by Rajai Davis. The Cubs limped into extra innings battling not only the Indians' momentum, but also the weather. A 17-minute rain delay ignited fears that the game might not get finished that night. During the intermission, Cubs players gathered in the Progressive Field weight room for a meeting, during which Jason Heyward and other veteran leaders fired up the team and reminded them how far they had come.

Whether it was the inspirational speeches, the rain delay allowing the team to reset or divine intervention, the Cubs responded by putting a quick runner on base in the 10th on a Schwarber leadoff single. Albert Almora Jr. came in to pinch-run and showed great instincts, astutely tagging up to second on a

The top of the Cubs order listens to the national anthem prior to Game 1 in Cleveland.

In the first two rounds of the postseason, Kris Bryant hit .333 with one homer and six RBI.

In 2016, Jon Lester pitched in his third career World Series. He won the previous two with Boston in 2007 and 2013.

deep fly out to right-center by Bryant. Shaw then intentionally walked Rizzo. That's when Zobrist logged one of the biggest hits of his career, sending a ball just past third baseman Ramirez into the left-field corner for a run-scoring double. Miguel Montero followed that up two batters later with an RBI single to give the Cubs an 8-6 lead heading into the final half inning of their season.

"Most teams would have folded in that moment where we lost that lead," Zobrist said. "Hats off to J-Hey and Rossy and our other leaders for just making that moment happen and kind of turning the page for us. Then you get Schwarber coming up after the break, and he gets a big hit right away, and you feel like it's on, and we're going to do this."

Though Edwards allowed one run after getting two quick outs in the bottom of the 10th, Montgomery closed things out, inducing a weak Michael Martinez groundout to Bryant to end the 8-7 game and kick off a celebration a century in the making.

"I know so many people who are thinking of their grandfathers and fathers now in Chicago, and that's what it's all about," said Cubs Executive Vice President and General Manager Jed Hoyer. "It's bigger than these 25 guys. It's bigger than this organization. It's about this city and the fans who have stuck by this team forever."

After 108 years, Cubs players finally got to mob the pitcher's mound, creating indelible images fans will treasure for at least the next century. The back-and-forth Game 7 was immediately deemed a classic, with the Cubs delivering a comeback for the ages. ◑

Veteran catcher David Ross makes a tough play against the netting behind home plate on a Lonnie Chisenhall pop-up to end the first inning of Game 1.

Addison Russell was a force on both offense and defense for the Cubs in the World Series.

Ben Zobrist gets things going in the second inning of Game 1 with a double to center field off Corey Kluber.

Willson Contreras gets locked in before making his first career World Series start in Game 2.

David Ross, Chris Coghlan and Joe Maddon share a laugh before Game 2.

> "*Baseball is a crazy game. It will do crazy things to you, but this is the moment that we all look for when we were little kids, to play in the World Series and win it. We just took a small step [in Game 2], but we've still got a long way to go.*"
>
> — KYLE SCHWARBER —

After missing most of the season, Kyle Schwarber celebrates his first RBI of 2016. He went 2-for-4 with two RBI in Game 2.

Ben Zobrist points to the sky after Kyle Schwarber's RBI single in the third inning of Game 2.

Game 2 starter Jake Arrieta gave up just two hits in 5.2 innings to even the World Series 1-1.

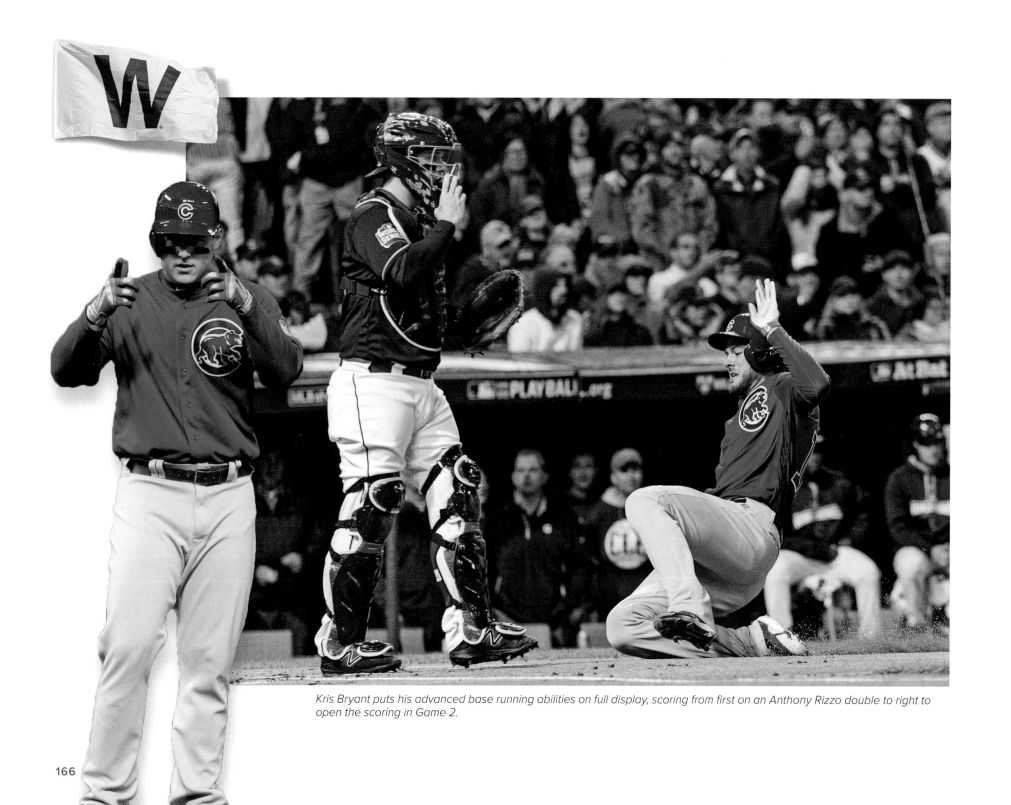

Kris Bryant puts his advanced base running abilities on full display, scoring from first on an Anthony Rizzo double to right to open the scoring in Game 2.

Mike Montgomery picks up where starter Jake Arrieta left off, twirling two scoreless innings of relief in the Cubs' 5-1 Game 2 win.

NUVEEN

WINTRUST

WRIGLEYROOFTOPS.COM

PLEASE WELCOME WAYNE MESSMER

TOYOTA

WORLD SERIES

Wayne Messmer opens the proceedings at Wrigley Field. The Cubs pulled into Game 3 tied 1-1 in the series.

Fans gather outside Wrigley Field to see the first World Series game played at the ballpark since 1945.

WRIGLEY FIELD
HOME OF
CHICAGO CUBS
INDIANS VS. CUBS
WORLD SERIES GAME 3 | 7:00 PM
TOYOTA

Javier Baez works out with John Mallee before Game 3.

Kyle Schwarber, Anthony Rizzo and Chris Coghlan keep things loose in the clubhouse with some Nintendo 64. Mario Kart was a hit among the group.

Joe Maddon takes it all in from the bottom step of the Cubs dugout prior to the Game 3 introductions.

Game 3 starter Kyle Hendricks throws the first World Series pitch at Wrigley Field in 71 years.

Jorge Soler hustles into third base for a two-out triple in the seventh inning of Game 3.

Actor and comedian Bill Murray does a Daffy Duck impression while he conducts the seventh-inning stretch.

Fans in the Budweiser Bleachers try to get the Cubs going during Game 3.

The Cubs entered Game 4 in a 2-1 series hole at Wrigley Field.

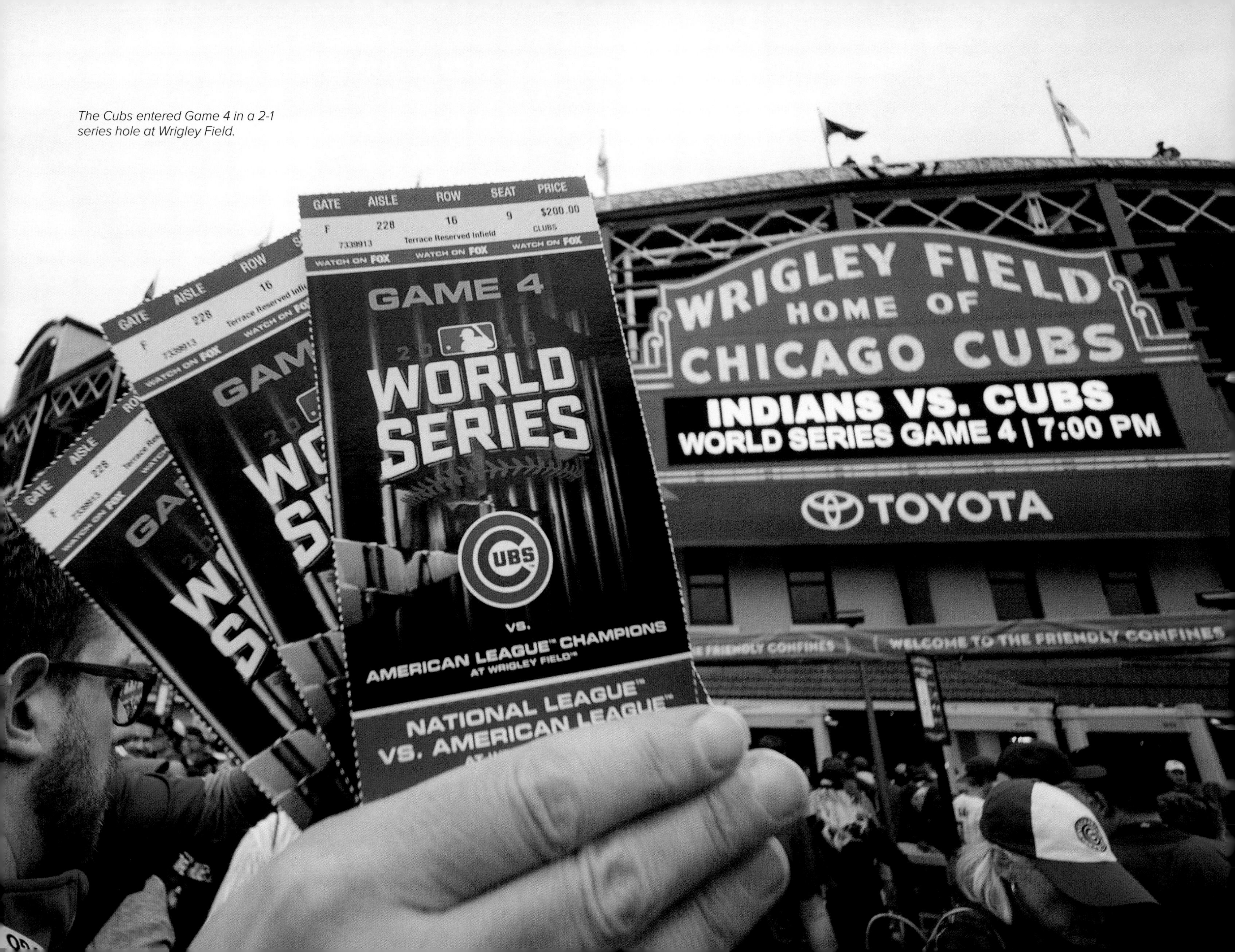

David Ross and his teammates joke around with strength and conditioning coordinator Tim Buss during batting practice.

Comedian Bill Murray sits with Hall of Famers Billy Williams, Greg Maddux and Fergie Jenkins prior to Game 4.

Julianna Zobrist sings "God Bless America" before her husband, Ben, takes the field for Game 4.

John Lackey surrendered three runs (two earned) in five innings in his final start of 2016. His 23 career postseason starts were the most among active pitchers through 2016.

Despite Anthony Rizzo's RBI single in the first, the Cubs dropped Game 4 by a score of 7-2.

Addison Russell turns a slick double play in the third inning of Game 4.

Despite the Game 4 loss, Dexter Fowler's eighth-inning homer off of Indians star reliever Andrew Miller showed the team had plenty of fight left.

After catcher David Ross tracks down a pop-up near the Indians dugout steps, first baseman Anthony Rizzo is there to scoop up the bobble and record the out in the second inning of Game 5.

Kris Bryant gets the offense going with a fourth-inning solo shot to left to tie Game 5 at 1-1.

David Ross comes up big with a fourth-inning sacrifice fly that would eventually be the difference in Game 5.

Javier Baez puts the tag on Indians shortstop Francisco Lindor after a perfect David Ross throw to end the top of the sixth inning.

Javier Baez runs off the field after applying the tag to catch Francisco Lindor stealing in the sixth inning of Game 5.

Gold Glove right fielder Jason Heyward battles the wind to haul in a fly ball along the right-field wall in Game 5.

In six career World Series appearances, Game 5 starter Jon Lester owns a 4-1 record and a 1.77 ERA.

Closer Aroldis Chapman comes in to preserve a 3-2 Cubs win in Game 5 to send the series back to Cleveland.

The Cubs celebrate winning their final game at Wrigley Field in 2016.

Anthony Rizzo shows off some moves in the clubhouse celebration room after Game 5.

Jake Arrieta makes his final appearance of 2016 count, striking out nine batters in 5.2 innings of work in Game 6.

Kris Bryant doesn't wait long to get the scoring started, homering in the top of the first inning of Game 6.

Anthony Rizzo high fives third base coach Gary Jones after Ben Zobrist moves him to third with a first-inning single.

Ben Zobrist collides with catcher Roberto Perez to score on Addison Russell's two-run double.

Addison Russell puts the game out of reach with a third-inning grand slam, giving the Cubs a 7-0 lead.

Despite struggling with the bat, Gold Glover Jason Heyward continued to flash the leather all postseason.

Addison Russell's six RBI in Game 6 tied a World Series record for RBI in a game. The Cubs would force Game 7 with a 9-3 win.

Aroldis Chapman comes into Game 6 with two outs in the seventh to face the heart of the Indians order.

GAME 7

WORLD SERIES

Indians

NATIONAL LEAGUE CHAMPIONS

AMERICAN LEAGUE VS. NATIONAL LEAGUE

GAME 7

*Progressive Field in Cleveland
gears up for the decisive Game 7.*

Kris Bryant focuses on the task at hand during batting practice prior to Game 7.

Joe Maddon appeared in his second career World Series as manager. His first was in 2008 with Tampa Bay.

It took all of four pitches for the Cubs to jump out to a 1-0 lead in Game 7 of the World Series, as leadoff man Dexter Fowler homers to center.

For the third consecutive postseason game, Kyle Hendricks picks off an opposing base runner.

Pitching in the biggest game of his career, Kyle Hendricks gave up one earned run in 4.2 innings of work and was in control for most of his start.

Kris Bryant slides underneath the tag to score on Addison Russell's fourth-inning sacrifice fly in Game 7.

Playing in the final game of his career, David Ross launches a sixth-inning solo shot to add to the Cubs' lead in Game 7.

> *Hey, whatever we've got to do. I mean, this time of year, there's no barriers. There's no nothing. It's all hands on deck.*
>
> — JON LESTER —

Making his first relief appearance since 2007, Jon Lester pitched three strong innings in the Game 7 win.

Despite a relatively quiet series, Javier Baez knocks opposing starter Corey Kluber out of the game with a fifth-inning homer.

Aroldis Chapman waits out the 17-minute rain delay following the ninth inning. He gave up three runs in the bottom of the eighth, but he worked through the ninth to get the Cubs into extra innings.

The Indians grounds crew removes the tarp before the 10th inning in Cleveland.

Ben Zobrist pushes a ball down the third-base line for a double, scoring Albert Almora Jr. from second in the top of the 10th inning of Game 7.

Anthony Rizzo stands on third base in disbelief following Ben Zobrist's go-ahead double in the top of the 10th.

Anthony Rizzo throws his hands in the air after Michael Martinez grounds out in the 10th inning to end the World Series.

Cubs players rush the field as champions after Mike Montgomery records the final out of the 2016 season.

The Cubs are 2016 World Series champions.

"I love tradition. I think tradition is worth time mentally, and tradition is worth being upheld. But curses and superstitions are not."

— JOE MADDON —

Ben Zobrist is awarded the World Series MVP. He hit .357 with a .919 OPS in seven games.

Cubs Chairman Tom Ricketts hoists the Commissioner's Trophy in the clubhouse. Ricketts and his family purchased the team in 2009.

Joe Maddon enjoys his moment with the trophy.

Champagne sprays all over the clubhouse following the trophy presentation.

Jake Arrieta douses his teammates in the victorious clubhouse.

Business executives Crane Kenney, Colin Faulkner, Jon Greifenkamp and Alex Sugarman take it all in at Progressive Field. The Cubs flew all associates to Cleveland for the World Series games.

Jed Hoyer, Theo Epstein and Jason McLeod, who all came to Chicago in 2011, proudly hold up the W flag.

Hall of Famer Ryne Sandberg celebrates on the field after the Cubs' Game 7 win.

Wrigley Field's brick exterior wall becomes a shrine to the Cubs' World Series title.

The corner of Clark and Addison erupts with Cubs fans following the win.

> *It's just so emotional. I hit a home run in Game 7 and got carried off the field. I mean, that doesn't happen. It was like Rudy going out there.*
>
> — DAVID ROSS —

Anthony Rizzo and Jason Heyward carry retiring catcher David Ross off the field for the final time.

Cubs president Crane Kenney said he hopes the chalk wall becomes an annual postseason tradition.

Members of the Cubs baseball operations team share a moment with the Commissioner's Trophy on the flight back to Chicago after Game 7 of the World Series.

Anthony Rizzo escorts the trophy home to Chicago.

WORLD CHAMPION
TROPHY TOUR

THE CUBS TAKE A WELL-EARNED
VICTORY LAP AFTER THE TITLE

It had been 108 years between World Series titles for the Cubs. When fans finally got a chance to celebrate their championship team, they were more than ready.

On Nov. 4, 2016, players, front-office personnel, alumni and family members boarded a caravan of double-decker tour buses and trolleys to take a victory lap around the city. Countless raucous, Cubbie blue-clad fans packed the streets surrounding Wrigley Field, the unofficial starting point for the parade, on a glorious early-November morning.

The fleet of buses moved onto Lake Shore Drive, which overlooks both Lake Michigan and the city's skyline, and then exited onto Michigan Avenue, entering a downtown corridor covered with both confetti and fans. The city of Chicago estimated 5 million people lined the parade route—the seventh-largest gathering of humanity in recorded history and the largest in U.S. history—culminating at Hutchinson Field in Grant Park for the championship rally.

"When I used to go to the minor-league clubhouses a few years ago, I would tell people that the men who are on the field when the Cubs win the World Series will not just be Chicago baseball players, but they're going to be Chicago baseball legends," said Cubs Chairman Tom Ricketts, the first person brought up to the podium by play-by-play radio announcer Pat Hughes, emcee for the afternoon's festivities.

Next up was President of Baseball Operations Theo Epstein, who stepped to the mic to a chorus of "TH-EO, TH-EO!" chants.

"I've been here for five years, and we've asked a lot of you," Epstein said. "We've put you through a lot these last five years—101 losses, trading players you've come to know and love for guys you've never heard of, trading 40 percent of the rotation three years in a row, asking you guys to follow the draft [and] follow the minor leagues. Let's be honest, for a while there, we forgot the 'not' in 'try not to suck.' But you stayed with us."

Manager Joe Maddon, sporting a "we did not suck" T-shirt under his Cubs jersey and a championship winter hat, came to the stage next, Commissioner's Trophy in hand. Like everyone else on the dais, he was impressed by the massive turnout.

"Welcome to Cubstock 2016. Look at this thing," he said, referring to the 1969 music festival in Woodstock, New York. He then praised his staff, calling it the best in baseball and lauding his coaches' tireless work ethic and preparation prior to each game.

Finally, Hughes announced the players. Somehow the already euphoric crowd had saved two of the loudest cheers for last. Star first baseman Anthony Rizzo stepped to the mic and thanked his teammates and their family members before tearing up and turning things over to beloved retiring catcher David Ross.

"He taught me a lot, personally, how to be a real winner," Rizzo said of Ross, whose career came to an end after Game 7 of the World Series. "He's like a brother, and he's taught me a lot in life, on the field and off the field. How to be a better person, and I'm forever grateful for him. He's going down a champion forever."

The raucous party came to an end when Rizzo handed Ricketts the game ball used for the final out of the World Series. This was a celebration more than a century in the making, and the city of Chicago definitely made the most of it. The Cubs were finally world champions and the class of baseball again.

But that was hardly the end of the festivities, as Cubs personnel enjoyed many of the new opportunities available to them. In the months following the parade, players made appearances on *Ellen*, *Saturday Night Live*, *The Tonight Show* and more. The team capped off its victory lap in style in Washington D.C. Just days before President and adopted Chicagoan Barack Obama left office in January, the Cubs made a pilgrimage to the White House. Though Obama is a White Sox fan, his wife, Michelle, is a lifelong Cubs supporter.

"Do know that among Sox fans, I am the Cubs' No. 1 fan," Obama remarked. ◉

The World Series and MVP trophies overlook the Cubs' victory rally.

> *It's really a team effort. A lot of people use that. They like the figurative sense. I mean it in the literal sense.*
>
> — TOM RICKETTS —

Laura, Todd and Tom Ricketts pass Wrigley Field as the Cubs parade gets underway.

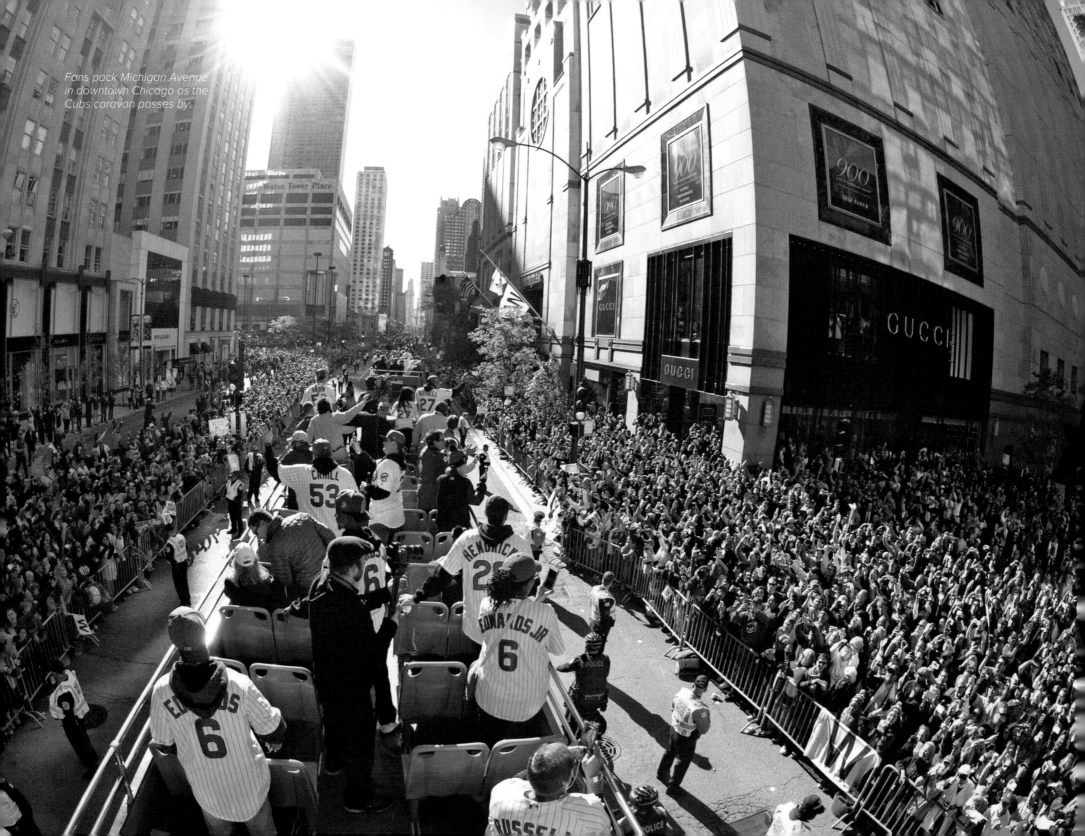

Fans pack Michigan Avenue in downtown Chicago as the Cubs caravan passes by.

Jake Arrieta flashes the W from his double-decker trolley.

Kyle Hendricks shows off the Commissioner's Trophy as the Cubs move through downtown Chicago.

FLY THE W

WORLD SERIES CHAMPIONS

#FlyThe W

es

The baseball operations staff enjoys its day in the sun.

Addison Russell and Justin Grimm salute the downtown Chicago crowd.

The Cubs parade winds its way through Chicago.

Kyle Schwarber salutes fans on boats in the Chicago River, which was dyed blue to mark the occasion.

773 648 5000 · www.chicagodoubledecker.com

13527 PT

The parade and rally are believed to be the largest public gathering in U.S. history.

Anthony Rizzo hands Cubs Chairman Tom Ricketts the game ball used for the final out of the World Series.

The Cubs starting rotation of Jason Hammel, Jon Lester, Jake Arrieta, Kyle Hendricks and John Lackey was the best in baseball in 2016.

Country star and Cubs fan Brett Eldredge leads the crowd in a stirring rendition of "Go Cubs Go."

Dexter Fowler, Anthony Rizzo, Jon Lester and David Ross sing along to "Go Cubs Go."

The Cubs bring it in one last time to wrap up the afternoon's festivities.

Confetti rains down on the Cubs World Series parade and rally in Chicago.

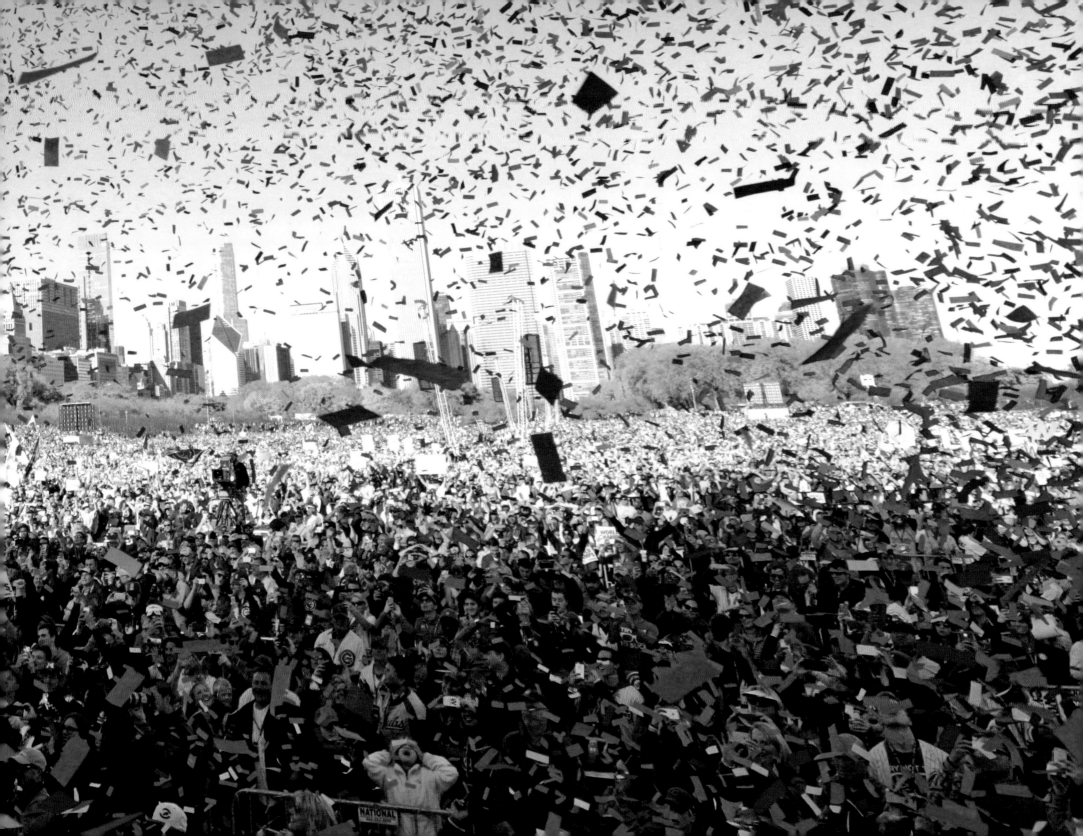

Javier Baez, singer Leslie Grace and Aroldis Chapman present the award for best tropical fusion album at the 17th annual Latin Grammy Awards.

South Carolina native Carl Edwards Jr. swings away during the Carolina Panthers' "Keep Pounding" ceremony prior to a Thursday night NFL game.

Kris Bryant and David Ross talk with Ellen DeGeneres about dancing on Saturday Night Live and experiencing the World Series parade in Chicago.

© 2016 NBCUNIVERSAL MEDIA, LLC   PHOTO BY DANA EDELSON/NBC/NBCU PHOTO BANK VIA GETTY IMAGES

"I feel like good guys finish first. Being humble and just being a good role model for kids out there —that's something I strive for more than putting up good numbers on the field."

— KRIS BRYANT —

Anthony Rizzo, David Ross and Dexter Fowler prepare to harmonize with Bill Murray on Saturday Night Live.

Kyle Schwarber gets a little on-air work behind the plate with Kelly Ripa on Live with Kelly.

Led by Theo Epstein, the Cubs applaud President Barack Obama during the team's visit to the White House on Jan. 16.

President Barack Obama shows off his new Cubs jersey.

The Cubs celebration was President Barack Obama's last official White House event.

Over the last few years, W flags have become a tradition at Cubs games, both at home and on the road. Fans have carried the W flag all over the world to show their support for the team.

HEY! CHICAGO
YOU W ON OVER THIS FAN ONCE
YOU W ON OVER US FANS ONCE
YOU W ON OVER ALL NATION
ONCE AGAIN! ITS BEEN A LONG
LONG TIME! 1908 2016

FLY THE W ™

–Dawn Mowka, Afghanistan

–Paul V. Howard, Breckenridge, Colorado

–Morton and Miriam Steinberg, Antarctica

–Alan Baldwin, Ridge Farm, Illinois

–Joe Cacchione, Sydney, Australia

—Armando Sanchez, Vatican City

—Squinn34, Universal Theme Park, Orlando, Florida

—Bob Bennett, Baghdad, Iraq

—Susan Elkins, Paris, France

—Brad Nolan, Pyramids of Giza, Cairo, Egypt

JOE MADDON

I have now had some time to reflect on the Cubs winning their first World Series title in 108 years, and I still haven't processed all that's happened yet. Almost everything about this year was different—from the goal of delivering a moment fans had been anticipating for so long, to being the steward of this particular group, to the role I've played here in Chicago. All of it was unique and special.

It's taken me a while to get to this point. On so many different levels, I'm grateful it took me so long to get my first major-league managerial job. I firmly believe everything I've learned was well worth the time. I feel totally prepared for almost every situation now, and I really owe it to my minor-league training and my scouting development. I mean that sincerely. I really believe that everybody should have the same opportunities I've had to go from step one to step two, without skipping anything in between. When you do it that way, I think you're better prepared for a lot of different moments. I'm very grateful for that.

Most places I've been in my career, I've been a part of the heavy lifting. Here, the heavy lifting was already done by the time I arrived. It was just up to me to create the culture. And trust me when I say I know how lucky I am to be with this organization.

Since I've been here—but especially this season—the diversity and the unity have made the experience so special. There is a great combination of young and old, experience and inexperience. The experienced guys handled their roles perfectly, and the younger guys did the same. They accepted constructive criticism well. They didn't cower from it. They took the information and literally ran with it. But the guys giving the information were also a great influence. There are times when you get veteran players who can actually make a negative impact on a group. Our guys made a positive impact, which is what created the unity. It was a bunch of young guys with a bunch of older brothers. That interaction was spectacular to watch.

It's not easy to be in the cross-hairs all season long. That was why I rolled out the "embrace the target" mantra this spring. Why deny it? We are good. People think we're going to win the World Series. Everybody is going to be coming after us. When I initially said embrace the target, my bigger concern was matching up against the teams that weren't considered as good. When you are the target, second-division teams are going to play their best games against you because they want to beat the best.

Really, that whole philosophy is rooted in a Tom Clancy novel. In *Clear and Present Danger*, Jack Ryan is an advisor to the president, and there is a drug deal gone bad in the Caribbean. As it turns out, it involved the president's friend. The spin doctors wanted him to say he hardly knew the guy, but Jack Ryan said, "No, Mr. President. He was not only your friend, he was your best friend." In other words, he wanted the president to run toward the problem to disarm it. I thought by really embracing the situation—admitting to it, knowing it, not running away from it—we had our best chance to overcome it. I wanted our players to know that "pressure" and "expectations" are actually positive, synonymous words. Why wouldn't you want to play with championship expectations? That's what we're all here for.

What was going through my head during that final play in Game 7 was pretty simple: "Catch it, Rizz. Please catch it." When Kris Bryant slipped, I thought, "Oh, no. This ball may go over Rizz's head." But then Bryant put it right in Rizzo's face, and Rizz caught it. My first thought in a moment like that is usually about the coaches and what it means to them, but this time I thought about 108 years. I don't know why, but I did. I knew how significant this was going to be to everybody affiliated with the Cubs, whether that's ownership, front office, players, families of anybody within the organization or fans. This was a worldwide event. It was all-consuming on a much larger scale than anything I've ever been a part of.

The parade, honestly, I have not sat down and processed yet. Wow. I knew it was going to be a parade, but I didn't know it was going to be that kind of a parade. I didn't know the folks would turn out like that. I've only been in the National League for two years, so I never really understood the scope of it until I got here. Every place I've gone, it's incredible. I can't go anywhere right now because everybody watched, everybody was a Cubs fan. Even if they weren't, they jumped on for a brief moment. I think maybe five or 10 years from now, I might really get it. But for right now, I'm just extremely gratified and happy.

If there's one thing you should know about these 2016 Cubs, it's that these guys are truly authentic. This is a group of authentic people. That's what I think really resonates with fans, and I also believe it's why the team was able to come back from a three to one deficit in the World Series. They are authentic. There is no hyperbole among them. There is not any kind of false hustle among them. They're just real people, and they're still really young. That's the other part about this. Everybody kept saying how great we were. I'm here to tell you, there are a lot of guys on that team who aren't even close to being as good as they're going to be. That's definitely something to look forward to.

This is a group of authentic young people, and they're very unified. That's why we won. I feel lucky to have been a part of it. Now it's time to start thinking about next year.

Joe Maddon

— Joe Maddon

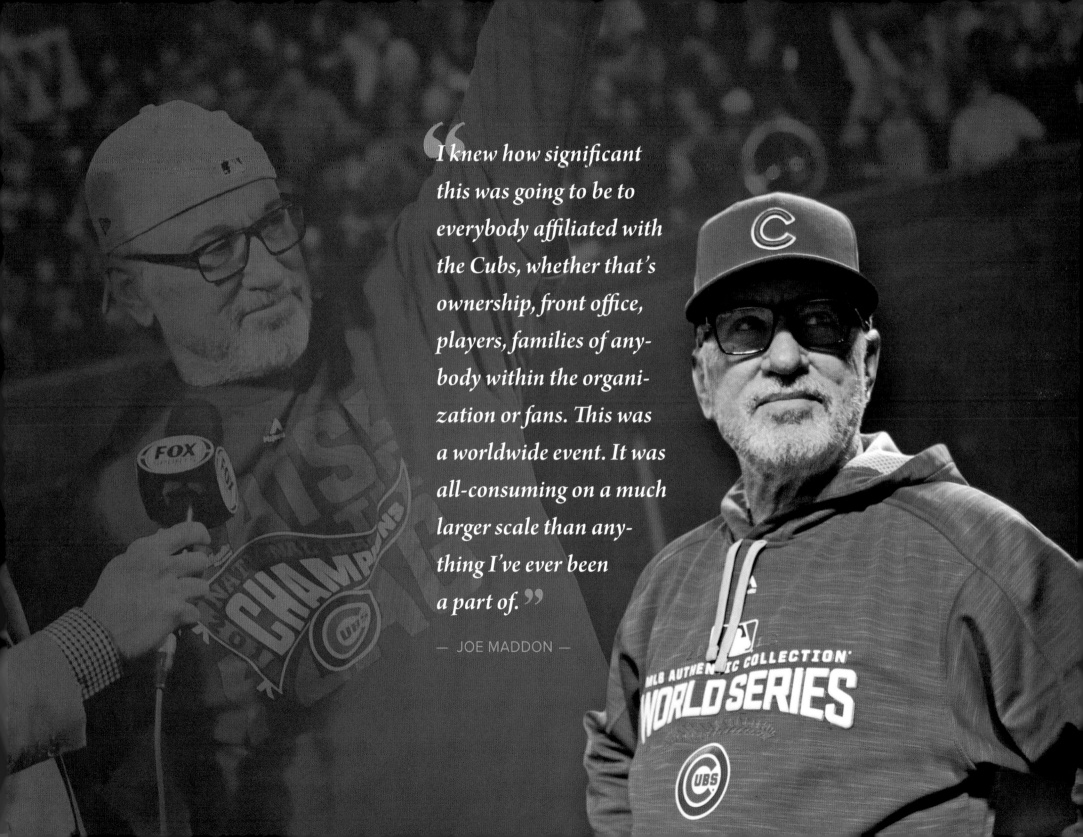

> "I knew how significant this was going to be to everybody affiliated with the Cubs, whether that's ownership, front office, players, families of anybody within the organization or fans. This was a worldwide event. It was all-consuming on a much larger scale than anything I've ever been a part of."

— JOE MADDON —

After parts of three seasons as the Phillies' manager, Hall of Famer Ryne Sandberg returned to the Cubs in 2016 as an ambassador.

"The World Series victory meant so much more to me personally than I ever thought it would. Until I was able to be there and experience it, I had no idea the impact it would have on me. It was life changing. I know I didn't play a game in 2016, but I felt like a winner and a world champion for the first time. It blew me away."

— RYNE SANDBERG —

RYNE SANDBERG

When Kris Bryant threw that ball to Anthony Rizzo to end Game 7 in Cleveland, my reaction was probably the same as yours. I jumped up and down, I yelled, I hugged my family, and I high-fived all the Cubs fans around me. It was over. The Cubs were World Series champions.

And then I looked around in disbelief. It happened. It really happened. Finally.

I had been waiting for that day since the moment I learned I had been traded to the Cubs in 1982. I had a couple of chances as a player, in 1984 and 1989, but we fell short. It was always my greatest regret that we couldn't deliver a championship for Cubs fans.

Every year of my career, that's what we were trying to do. Every winter working out, every spring training getting ready and every summer as we played the games, that was always our focus. We went into each season wanting to win the World Series. Sadly, we never got there.

I accomplished some great things during my career. I won an MVP Award. I won the home run title. I made 10 All-Star Games. I made it to the Hall of Fame.

These are all great accomplishments, but I couldn't have done any of those things without my teammates, and ultimately what you play for is to win with your teammates. That's the greatest joy there is in sports.

Driving to Cleveland for Game 1 of the World Series, I could hardly sit still. I was trying to picture what it was going to be like to participate in the Fall Classic for the first time—to see it up close and personal and to be so invested in the team I've been with since I was 21 years old. It was hard to believe it was actually happening. This is something I dreamed about with my teammates for so many years, being that first Cubs team to make it to the World Series since 1945. I just wanted to be involved with the organization, and, fortunately for me, I got to be a part of it.

Game 3 at Wrigley Field was surreal. I was at the park at 6 a.m. to do the local TV morning shows, and it was still dark outside. I walked down the aisle and stopped before heading onto the field. I saw the World Series logos on the first-base and third-base sides and saw the bunting around the stadium. I soaked it all in. A World Series game was going to be played that night at Wrigley Field. I shook my head, smiled and just tried to come to grips with that reality.

When we went down three games to one, I reflected back on the 2016 team I watched for the entire regular season and throughout the first two rounds of the postseason. I really thought the pitching was lined up for the next three games, and I had a good feeling about the outcome. The season was full of magical moments, and there was something different about this group of players, especially their character and the joy they got from playing baseball—something I really appreciate. I was so impressed with them that I truly felt they were going to get it done.

I had the honor of throwing out the first pitch on Sunday before Game 5, and it was a great feeling being out on the field. The crowd was electric. I thought it was my duty to get them rolling that night.

We won Game 5, the last game of 2016 at Wrigley Field. I would be remiss if I didn't point out how much fun I had at the Friendly Confines in 2016. I saw about 70 regular-season games from the stands, and it was a blast celebrating wins with family, friends and Cubs fans all summer long.

After winning Game 6, there was no doubt in my mind we would win Game 7. The final out was a celebration. My family and I were surrounded by Cubs fans in the stands, and it was pure jubilation. High-fives, screams, hugs and tears. "Yes, we did it!" is all I could think.

The World Series victory meant so much more to me personally than I ever thought it would. Until I was able to be there and experience it, I had no idea the impact it would have on me. It was life changing. I know I didn't

play a game in 2016, but I felt like a winner and a world champion for the first time. It blew me away.

Now the past is just the past. We can enjoy the wins, and we don't have to live with the disappointments. It was a chance for me to turn the page on the perception of the Cubs, and it erases all talk of curses or foul balls or any of the other excuses used for losing in the past.

It forever lifted a weight off my shoulders and off the shoulders of so many alumni who now look at themselves as part of a world championship. From here, the question is only about how many titles the Cubs can win.

I'm so grateful to Tom Ricketts, Crane Kenney, Theo Epstein and Jed Hoyer for bringing me back into the fold; to Jason McLeod and Joe Maddon for making me feel like a part of the team; and to the players, coaches and staff members for welcoming me with open arms.

The Chicago Cubs are World Series champions, and we never again have to answer the question about when, or if, it will ever happen. On behalf of the great Cubs fans all over the world and all of my former teammates, coaches and managers during my career in Chicago, thank you to the 2016 Cubs players. You have made our dreams come true.

*23
HOF '05*

—Ryne Sandberg

Hall of Famer and Cubs legend Billy Williams throws out the first pitch at Game 3 of the World Series at Wrigley Field.

BILLY WILLIAMS

First and foremost, what this World Series title means to me is that I won't have to go around the city and hear, "Will the Cubs ever win it in my lifetime?" anymore. I've heard that so often from people I've encountered over the years. A lot of that went away after last year's postseason run. The young ballplayers' efforts seemed to ease fans worries a bit. And, of course, after they won 103 games in 2016, I knew the team was on its way.

As for the World Series games themselves, they were so exciting. We were down three games to one, and then we came back to tie up the series and win it. We won the World Series. I was watching it on television, and when I saw Kris Bryant pick that ball up on the final out, I said, "Make a good throw. Make a good throw!" When he threw the ball and Anthony Rizzo caught it and I watched him put that baseball in his back pocket, I said, "Holy cow, we won a World Series!" Since 1908, we haven't been there—108 years, we haven't been there.

So it was exciting for my family and for me. We were all sitting around watching the game, and I'll tell you, it was a joyous time

> **"The 2016 Chicago Cubs winning the World Series will forever be etched in stone. This won't happen again. No franchise will go 108 years without winning a World Series title."**

because so many people through the years have suffered. There are fans—not only here in Chicago, but all over the world—who were watching in support of their team. The Chicago Cubs have picked up a lot of fans throughout the years because they have long been the underdog story.

I can say "we" did it. Not only did they do it, but we did it. I get emotional because I think of so many guys who played in this organization and who were here performing for the Chicago

Cubs, and all of the previous players who wanted that trophy so bad. I guarantee you those guys got just as much of a thrill out of winning as the players on the field today. Throughout the years, we were always considered the doormat of the National League, and now we don't have to be called that anymore. We're winners here in Chicago, and you've got some winning athletes on this ball team.

The World Series win also gives me great satisfaction because it allows me to think about my compadres Ernie Banks and Ron Santo. It would have been nice to have been able to watch these games with Santo because we played together for so many years. We started out in 1959 together, and in all those years we played together, I was always hitting third while he hit fourth. When we both came up, Ernie was huge. For so many years, we played together, and we were a part of each other's lives. If they had been around to witness what has happened, we would have talked about it for days.

When the Cubs won, I really thought about those guys. I thought about those guys and how it would have been to celebrate with them—three guys who were here for so, so long and tried so hard to bring a pennant to Chicago.

As new players came into the organization over the years, I made sure to tell each and every one of them how special it would be to be a member of the team that wins the World Series here with the Chica-

go Cubs—especially those guys who came up through the minors and have been around the organization for a while and have gotten a true feeling for the culture of the club. I'd tell them they were going to be bigger than the Bulls were when they won. They were going to be bigger than the 1985 Bears. People will remember them forever because of how long everybody has waited. And we've put together a young, talented ballclub with good chemistry that's full of guys who want to be here and want to play and perform for 42,000 people every day. They've made it a thrill just to walk into that ballpark.

The 2016 Chicago Cubs winning the World Series will forever be etched in stone. This won't happen again. No franchise will go 108 years without winning a World Series title. The interworkings of the game and sports' evolution won't let that happen again, and that's what has made this one of the most special spectacles in the world. It's etched in stone. This will always be there. The Cubs won the World Series. Say that again—the Cubs won the World Series.

And now we celebrate.

Billy Williams #26
H.O.F. '87

—Billy Williams

> *"When the Cubs won, I really thought about [Ernie Banks and Ron Santo]. I thought about those guys and how it would have been to celebrate with them—three guys who were here for so, so long and tried so hard to bring a pennant to Chicago."*
>
> — BILLY WILLIAMS —

Members of the Cubs coaching staff and baseball operations department celebrate their World Series title.

PAT HUGHES

I received many compliments from people telling me how much they enjoyed my call when the Cubs clinched the National League pennant for the first time since 1945. They all said they enjoyed that I didn't try to do too much and that I took a nice, long pause to let the moment breathe after the final out.

People thought I was taking that pause to be dramatic, but let me be honest: I needed to stop for a few seconds. I was doing it because it was such an emotionally overwhelming moment for me personally, as I think it was for Cubs fans everywhere. This was my 34th consecutive year as a big-league broadcaster, and it was going to be my first World Series behind the microphone.

The 2016 Cubs season was full of unforgettable moments. Even though the team was in control for much of the season, there were still plenty of games and sequences that are forever burned in my memory. Here are a few I'll never forget.

I think a significant series was when the Cubs swept three games in Pittsburgh in May and then came home to sweep four from Washington. After they went 7-0 against that level of competition, I knew this team was something special.

Another turning point for me was Anthony Rizzo's home run off the Mets' Steven Matz in a July 18 game at Wrigley Field. That homer came in the third inning, on the 10th pitch of the at-bat, after Rizzo had fought off multiple pitches to stay alive. The Mets had swept four in a row from the Cubs earlier in the month, after having swept the National League Championship Series the previous year. They seemed to have the Cubs' number. Rizzo's three-run homer early in the game gave the Cubs the lead. It was a lefty versus lefty. Rizzo fouled off seven or eight pitches, and then he just launched one into the bleachers in right-center. The Cubs went on to win that game and that series.

The single-most exciting moment of the regular season for me was the Cubs' dramatic comeback win in late July over Seattle, when Jon Lester came on as the unlikeliest of pinch-hitters and laid down a perfect bunt that drove in Jason Heyward for the game's winning run. The team went down big early but never gave up. I remember Joe Maddon said something like, "Boy, that's the kind of game that can put you on a good little stretch." Well, that began an 11-game winning streak that placed the Cubs squarely in the NL Central driver's seat.

After a hard-fought National League Division Series with the Giants, one of my fondest memories took place on our way home. We came back to Wrigley Field after the Game 4 win late in the night, and there were reporters from local television stations and fans outside the ballpark waiting for us. We hadn't even been to bed yet, and here they were interviewing us and congratulating us.

As the Cubs moved on to face the Dodgers in the National League Championship Series, things got even more difficult. I've got to be honest, when you're down two games to one in the NLCS, and you've got two more games as a road team, it's uncomfortable. You're not panicking, but it's not a good feeling. Dodger Stadium has never been an easy place for visiting teams to win, but the Cubs turned it around in Game 4.

I know it sounds corny—and people may not believe it—but I still get goose bumps just thinking about how, prior to Game 6, the Cubs had a chance to win the National League pennant. I am well aware that they are now the world champions, but at that time, they were still trying to win their first pennant in 71 years. I'll never forget the game Kyle Hendricks pitched that night. He was absolutely brilliant. The Cubs jumped on Kershaw early and scored a bunch of runs. Then, when Yasiel Puig bounced into the 6-4-3 double play, the roar at Wrigley Field was absolutely thunderous.

But that wasn't close to the most dramatic moment of the postseason. Just the thought of the 10th inning of Game 7 of the World Series still leaves me shaking with nerves. I love baseball history, and I love broadcasting history. You may not know this, but radio broadcasts of baseball weren't around in 1908. So for about the last month, I was thinking I could be the first person on a radio broadcast to ever say the words, "The Chicago Cubs win the World Series!" I was nervous, but I was excited.

As the game wore on, I was trying to concentrate on doing my job, which is easier said than done at a moment like that. It's at the end of Game 179, Game 7 of a World Series. It's the final inning of a four-and-a-half-hour, back-and-forth, marathon affair. At the age of 61, I was just battling and trying to hang in there as best I could. But I was pleased with the final call. I tell people all the time that in radio, you have to be true to that final call. You can never plan it out. If

> "Here's a grounder to short, the throw to second, the throw to first. The Cubs are going to the World Series! The Cubs win the pennant!"
>
> — PAT HUGHES —

Pat Hughes' scorecard for Game 7 of the World Series.

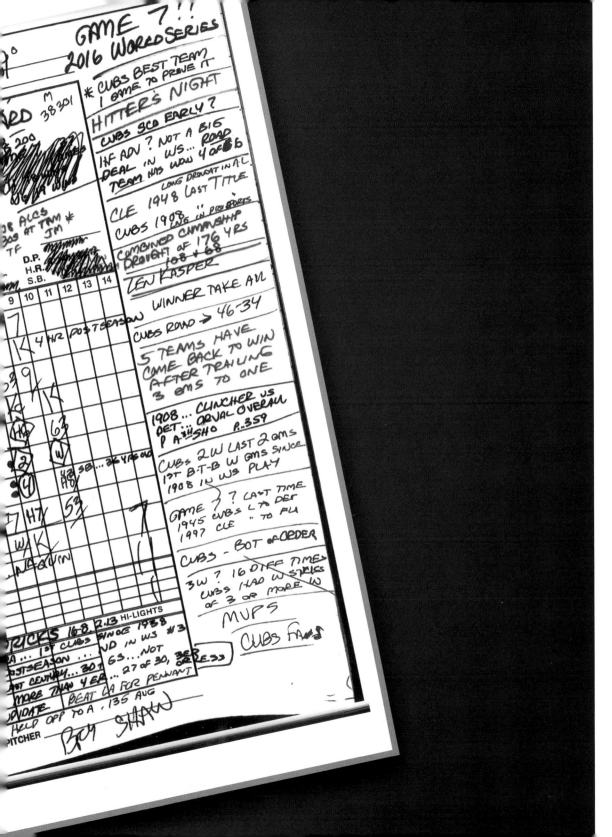

it's a definitive Cubs win, that's one feeling. If it's a dramatic, crazy, 10-inning game like we had, it's a whole different feeling. You've got to be true to the feeling and the moment.

I was thrilled at the World Series victory, not just for myself and the team, but also for Cubs fans everywhere. It was all really emotional. Ron Coomer and I both had tears in our eyes. Len Kasper was down on the field interviewing players on our postgame show, and that was emotional as well. Honestly, I spent a lot of time crying in the month following the postseason. And I'm more than OK with that.

We all knew the Cubs finally winning a World Series would be meaningful to this fan base, but I'm not sure anyone really understood just how much it would mean until it actually occurred. The last stretch of the season felt like it was happening to someone else. The World Series. The parade. I was also lucky enough to be nominated for the Ford C. Frick Award. These are amazing things that have occurred in succession, and to be honest, it has all been a little overwhelming.

To be able to etch my name into a moment in broadcasting history is something I'll always be thankful for. You never know where your career will lead, but I've always felt lucky to be a part of the Cubs family. To be behind the mic for the last out of the organization's first world championship in 108 years is more than I could have ever asked for.

I can't wait to see what the next few years have in store.

— Pat Hughes

The Cubs gather at Wrigley Field with the Commissioner's Trophy before the World Series parade and rally in Chicago.

The Chicago skyline is lit up in recognition of the Cubs' 2016 World Series title.

PHOTO CREDITS

PHOTOGRAPHER	PAGE(S)
STEPHEN GREEN/CHICAGO CUBS	V, X, XX, XXVI, XXVIII, 2, 3, 4, 5, 6, 7, 8, 9, 10, 13, 14, 15, 16, 17, 18, 19, 20, 21, 22, 26, 27, 28, 32, 33, 34, 35, 37, 38, 39, 40, 41, 43, 44, 45, 47, 48, 52, 54, 55, 56, 58, 62, 63, 64, 65, 66, 68, 69, 70, 71, 77, 78, 80, 82, 84, 85, 86, 87, 89, 94, 95, 97, 98, 99, 101, 104, 105, 106, 108, 112, 114, 115, 117, 119, 120, 121, 123, 124, 125, 127, 128, 129, 130, 131, 135, 136, 137, 143, 146, 147, 148, 150, 151, 153, 156, 157, 158, 159, 160, 163, 164, 165, 166, 167, 171, 172, 173, 175, 176, 181, 183, 184, 185, 186, 187, 189, 190, 191, 193, 194, 195, 196, 197, 198, 199, 200, 206, 207, 209, 212, 213, 215, 216, 217, 221, 227, 232, 233, 240, 244, 248, 251, 254, 259
ARMANDO L. SANCHEZ/GETTY	12
CAROLINA PANTHERS/GOODSTUFF CREATIVE	230
CAYLOR ARNOLD	141, 173
CHRIS BERNACCHI	VIII, 168, 202, 241
CHRISTIAN PETERSEN/GETTY	27
COURTESY CHICAGO CUBS	69, 209, 242
DAN MENDLIK	BACK COVER
DANA EDELSON/NBC/ NBCU PHOTO BANK VIA GETTY IMAGES	231
DAVID BANKS	2, 6, 25, 42, 81, 132
DAVID DUROCHIK	FRONT COVER, FRONT COVER INSIDE, II, XIII, XIV, 6, 7, 30, 64, 75, 88, 90, 91, 116, 118, 140, 143, 144, 145, 161, 176, 177, 178, 179, 188, 194, 201, 204, 208, 209, 218, 220, 225, 239
DAVID M. RUSSELL//DISNEY/ABC HOME ENTERTAINMENT AND TV DISTRIBUTION ©2016 DISNEY ABC. ALL RIGHTS RESERVED	231
DENIS POROY/GETTY	51
DILIP VISHWANAT/GETTY	67
ELIZABETH PRATT	83, 110, 139
ERICK W. RASCO/GETTY	170
EZRA SHAW/GETTY	96
HARRY HOW/GETTY	51
JAMIE SABAU/GETTY	31
J. GEIL	XIX, 72, 73, 113, 138, 142, 143, 151, 154, 162, 173, 185, 192, 193, 199, 209, 211, 223, 239
JOE ROBBINS/GETTY	36
JOHN KONSTANTARAS	134, 144, 180, 219, 222, 224, 226, 228, 234
JONATHAN DANIEL/GETTY	58, 59
JON DURR/GETTY	60
JOSE MORE	XXIII
KEVIN SAGHY	14
KEVIN WINTER/WIREIMAGE	230
LG PATTERSON/GETTY	51
LOUIS REQUENA	247
MICHAEL ROZMAN	230
MICHAEL ZAGARIS	XVI, 92, 99, 100, 102, 103, 107
NANCY STONE/CHICAGO TRIBUNE/TNS	58
MICHAEL ZITO	122, 126, 127
ROBIN ALAM/GETTY	174
RON VESELY/GETTY	76, 174, 182
ROSS DETTMAN	XXIV, 210, 242, 247, 256
SEAN M. HAFFEY/GETTY	50

FLY THE W

The publisher has made all reasonable efforts to reach photographers and/or copyright owners of images used in this book. Any omission is entirely unintentional, and the publisher will be pleased to insert appropriate acknowledgement in any subsequent edition. The publisher is prepared to pay fair and reasonable fees for any usage made without compensation or agreement.